W9-BSE-684

Also by Robert Byrne

Nonfiction

McGoorty: A Pool Room Hustler

Byrne's New Standard Book of Pool and Billiards

Byrne's Treasury of Trick Shots in Pool and Billiards

Byrne's Advanced Technique in Pool and Billiards

Byrne's Wonderful World of Pool and Billiards

The 637 Best Things Anybody Ever Said

The Other 637 Best Things Anybody Ever Said

The Third—and Possibly the Best—637 Best Things Anybody Ever Said

The Fourth—and by Far the Most Recent—637 Best Things Anybody Ever Said

The Fifth and Far Finer Than the First Four 637 Best Things Anybody Ever Said

The 2,548 Best Things Anybody Ever Said

Writing Rackets

Cat Scan: All the Best from the Literature of Cats (editor)

Every Day Is Father's Day (editor)

Fiction

Thrill

Byrne's Book of Great Pool Stories

Mannequin

Skyscraper

Always a Catholic

The Dam

The Tunnel

Memories of a Non-Jewish Childhood

Essays

Behold My Shorts

THE 2,548 WITTIEST THINGS ANYBODY EVER SAID

SELECTED AND COMPILED BY

ROBERT BYRNE

A TOUCHSTONE BOOK
Published by Simon & Schuster
New York London Toronto Sydney New Delhi

Touchstone
A Division of Simon & Schuster, Inc.
1230 Avenue of the Americas
New York, NY 10020

First Touchstone trade paperback edition May 2012

TOUCHSTONE and colophon are registered trademarks of Simon & Schuster, Inc.

For information about special discounts for bulk purchases, please contact Simon & Schuster Special Sales at 1-866-506-1949 or business@simonandschuster.com.

The Simon & Schuster Speakers Bureau can bring authors to your live event. For more information or to book an event contact the Simon & Schuster Speakers Bureau at 1-866-248-3049 or visit our website at www.simonspeakers.com.

Manufactured in the United States of America

10 9 8 7 6 5 4

Library of Congress Cataloging-in-Publication Data

The 2,548 wittiest things anybody ever said / selected and compiled by Robert Byrne.
p. cm.
"A Touchstone book."
1. Quotations, English. 2. Wit and humor. I. Byrne, Robert, 1930–
PN6081.A129 2012
082—dc23

2011041236

ISBN 978-1-4516-4890-4
ISBN 978-1-4516-4891-1 (ebook)

Dedicated with love to my wife, Cindy,
who is one in a million or at least 500,000.

The day that is most completely wasted
is the one in which you did not laugh.

—*Chamfort (1741–1794)*

CONTENTS

INTRODUCTION

Two questions I'm often asked are (1) Who the hell do you think you are? and (2) What's the significance of the number 2,548 in the title of this book and your previous collection of quotations? This is neither the time nor the place to answer the first question, which will be addressed in a memoir I'm working on titled *Who the Hell I Think I Am.* I'll tackle the second question as briefly as possible because the answer is only minimally interesting.

My first collection of quotes came out in 1982 and was based on a notebook I had been keeping for a decade called "Remarks Worth Remembering." When there were enough good ones for a book, I counted them and found 637, so that number became part of the title. The book sold so well in both hardcover and paperback that there were sequels with similar titles . . . in 1984, 1986, and 1990. Are you good at arithmetic? Then it has already struck you that 4 times 637 is 2,548. An omnibus of the four 637s was published by Touchstone, an imprint of Simon & Schuster, in 2003, titled *The 2,548 Best Things Anybody Ever Said.*

Note that in the title of the present volume the word *wittiest* replaces *best.* True, the emphasis is more strongly on wit this time, but the earlier collection has a whole hell of a lot of witty one-liners. (Note to self: You also used *hell* in the first sentence. Take one out.) Lines such as the following would be in the book you hold if they weren't already in the 2003 collection:

"How can I believe in God when just last week I got my tongue caught in the roller of an electric typewriter?" (Woody Allen)

"The United States is like the guy at the party who gives everybody cocaine and still nobody likes him." (Jim Samuels)

"A terrible thing happened again last night—nothing." (Phyllis Diller)

"Losing my virginity was a career move." (Madonna)

"It's relaxing to go out with my ex-wife because she already knows I'm an idiot." (Warren Thomas)

"In breeding cattle, you need one bull for every twenty-five cows, unless the cows are known sluts." (Johnny Carson)

Are you the analytical type? Then you will notice that while the quotes are grouped by subject, the subjects aren't ordered according to the alphabet. When fitting, the subjects follow each other in a storylike progression. Sex follows Dating. Babies follow Marriage. Death follows Suicide. Boredom follows Lawyers. It's a quote book, therefore, that can be read from front to back.

Indexes of Sources, Authors, and Subjects and Key Words will help you give a talk, write a book, pretend to have a sense of humor, or locate a half-remembered line. It's a good bathroom book, too, but to make sure it is used for reading only, I must warn you that the paper and ink are highly toxic.

Turn elsewhere for uplift or inspiration, for the pompous and the dull. No effort was made to have a quote on every subject, from every famous person, or from every era. Humor, cleverness, and surprise were the main criteria.

Robert Byrne
Dubuque, Iowa

THE 2,548 WITTIEST THINGS ANYBODY EVER SAID

DATING

1

Men will sleep with women they wouldn't date, and women will date men they wouldn't sleep with.

—Rebecca Christian

2

I know we've only just met, but I have the feeling that I've known you all my life because every little thing you do drives me up the wall.

—Dan Piraro in his Bizarro *comic strip*

3

Rules for teenage dating: 1. Don't take the third drink. 2. Keep one foot on the floor.

—Sister Mary Xavier

4

I don't mind men who kiss and tell. I need all the publicity I can get.

—Ruth Buzzi

5

There are times not to flirt. When you're sick. When you're with children. When you're on the witness stand.

—Joyce Jillson (1945–2004)

6

I'm afraid of dating. When the guy shows up at the door, I give him my purse and beg him not to hurt me.

—Maria Bamford

7

When I'm in a wig, I'm pretty attractive. I stare at mirrors because I'm my type.

—Kevin McDonald

8

Relationships are based on trust until you meet someone new.

—Howard Stern

9

My girlfriend wants me to become a better person so I can get a better girlfriend.

—*Anthony Jeselnik*

10

Prince Charming doesn't come on a white horse anymore. He comes in a Honda and needs help with the payments.

—*Mary Wolfe*

11

There comes a time in a relationship when a man develops enough confidence and ease to bore you to death.

—*Eve Babitz*

12

Men are like jobs—they're easier to find if you already have one.

—*Paige Mitchell*

13

He looked at me as if I was a side dish he hadn't ordered.

—*Ring Lardner (1885–1933)*

14

How come so many women like horses, which are big and smelly and go to the toilet all over the place, and are highly critical when men exhibit the same qualities?

—Dave Barry

15

To attract men I wear a perfume called New Car Interior.

—Rita Rudner

16

I'm dating a homeless woman. It's easier to get her to stay over.

—Garry Shandling

17

A new survey shows that 55 percent of men pay for dinner on the first date. The other 45 percent have never had a second date.

—*Jimmy Fallon*

18

I think, therefore I'm single.

—*Liz Winston*

19

A man on a date wonders if he'll get lucky. The woman already knows.

—*Monica Piper*

20

My boyfriend called me by another name in bed. I said, "Who's Oprah?"

—*Jennifer Siegel*

21

You and I are a simply amazing couple. You're simple and I'm amazing.

—*Jim Fenney*

22

I've only dated one Asian girl, but she was very Asian. She was a panda.

—Jim Gaffigan

23

After two years I said to my boyfriend, "Tell me your name or it's over."

—Rita Rudner

24

If you suspect your date is deaf, it's a bad sign.

—Cynthia Heimel

25

How do you dump a guy who has disappeared?

—Cynthia Heimel

26

I always dated men for their height rather than for their wealth because . . . I wasn't thinking.

—Frances Dilorinzo

27

The difference between a job interview and a date is that at the end of a job interview there is not much chance that you'll end up naked.

—Jerry Seinfeld

28

The problem with my boyfriend is that I'm a night person and he's married.

—Wendy Liebman

29

I used to go out exclusively with actresses and other female impersonators.

—Mort Sahl

30

Whenever I want a really nice meal, I start dating again.

—Susan Healy

31

I've been on so many blind dates I should get a free dog.

—Wendy Liebman

32

In high school, my girlfriend's dad said, "I want my daughter back by eight fifteen." I said, "The middle of August? Cool!"

—Steven Wright

33

Employees make the best dates. You don't have to pick them up and they're deductible.

—Andy Warhol (1928–1987)

34

I dated a girl for two years and then the nagging started: "I wanna know your name!"

—Mikey Binder

35

Computer dating is great . . . if you're a computer.

—Rita Mae Brown

36

I believe in platonic friendships, but after, not before.

—John Copley (Lord Lyndhurst) (1772–1863)

37

Sleep with a guy once and before you know it he wants to take you to dinner.

—*Myers Yori*

38

A difference of taste in jokes is a great strain on the affections.

—*George Eliot (Mary Anne Evans, 1819–1880)*

39

My measurements are 37-24-38, but not necessarily in that order.

—*Carol Burnett*

40

I'm rich, you're thin. Together we're perfect.

—*B. Smaller*

41

I want a perfume that will overpower men. I'm sick of karate.

—Phyllis Diller

42

I dated a man for six months without realizing he was gay. I thought he was shy.

—Susan Richman

43

At about age thirty, most women think about having children, while men think about dating them.

—*Judy Carter*

44

Romance is thinking about the other person when you are supposed to be thinking of something else.

—*Roy Blount, Jr.*

45

When you're not blond and thin, you come up with a personality real fast.

—*Kathy Najimy*

46

Watch out for men who have mothers.

—*Laura Shapiro*

47

Not only was I not asked to the prom, nobody would tell me where it was.

—*Rita Rudner*

48

My girlfriend told me she was seeing another man. I told her to rub her eyes.

—*Emo Philips*

49

In bed, my girlfriend dresses me.

—*Richard Lewis*

50

If somebody makes me laugh, I'm his slave for life.

—*Bette Midler*

51

I'm lazy. I date pregnant women.

—*Ron Richards*

52

While waiting for Mr. Right, you can have a lot of fun with Mr. Wrong.

—*Cher*

53

Once a woman has forgiven her man, she must not reheat his sins for breakfast.

—Marlene Dietrich (1901–1992)

54

I got a sweater for Christmas. I was hoping for a screamer or a moaner.

—Unknown

55

I'm glad my girlfriend is a full-figured woman. If we lose the house, we can both live in her bloomers.

—Redd Foxx (1922–1991)

56

I see your face when I am dreaming;
That's why I always wake up screaming.

—Unknown

SEX

57

One dark and stormy night, a kiss rang out.

—*Snoopy (Charles Schulz, 1922–2000)*

58

A kiss is a lovely trick designed by nature to stop speech when words become superfluous.

—*Ingrid Bergman (1915–1982)*

59

In America, sex is an obsession—elsewhere it's a fact.

—*Marlene Dietrich (1901–1992)*

60

Foreplay is the palm before the storm.

—*Robert Byrne*

61

Millions of American women are married to men whose idea of foreplay is taking off their glasses.

—*Don Kaul*

62

I called a phone sex number and got a woman who stuttered. It cost me fifteen hundred bucks.

—*Johnny Rizzo*

63

Sex between a man and a woman can be wonderful, provided you get between the right man and woman.

—*Woody Allen*

64

I wish I got as much in bed as I get in the newspapers.

—Linda Ronstadt

65

I know body hair bothers some women, but a lot of men like a fluffy partner.

—Dame Edna Everage (Barry Humphries)

66

My last girlfriend was a prankster. When I opened the condom package, it turned out to be a moist towelette from Colonel Sanders.

—Dana Snow

67

I believe that sex is the most beautiful, natural, and wholesome thing money can buy.

—Steve Martin

68

I thought I told you to wait in the car.

—Tallulah Bankhead (1902–1968)
to a lover she hadn't seen in years

69

Sex is bad because it rumples the clothes.

—*Jackie Kennedy Onassis (1929–1994)*

70

My least favorite names for strippers are Edna, Bertha, Gertrude, and Walter.

—*Larry the Cable Guy (Daniel Lawrence Whitney)*

71

My high school was so small that Driver Education and Sex Education were taught in the same car.

—*Variously ascribed*

72

The last time I was inside a woman I was visiting the Statue of Liberty.

—*Woody Allen*

73

Never lie down with a woman who's got more troubles than you.

—*Nelson Algren (1909–1981)*

74

There are a number of mechanical devices that increase sexual arousal in women; chief among them is the Mercedes-Benz 380SL convertible.

—*P. J. O'Rourke*

75

Every woman learns to fake orgasm. It's common courtesy.

—*Joan Rivers*

76

Women can fake an orgasm, but men can fake a whole relationship.

—*Sharon Stone*

77

Sex is a dirty, disgusting act you save for someone you love.

—*Carol Henry's mother*

78

My boyfriend promised me that I was the only woman he would ever cheat on.

—*Merrill Markoe*

79

I wear fake fur. You'll never guess what I had to fake to get it.

—*Fran Drescher*

80

The best birth control is to make your husband sleep on the roof.

—*Margaret Sanger (1879–1966)*

81

The most effective birth control is to spend a day with my kids.

—*Jill Bensley*

82

Scientists have announced the invention of a woman's condom. It fits snugly over her wineglass.

—*Kevin Nealon*

83

Sex is God's charming apology for disease and death.

—*Jon Carroll*

84

The Tasmanians, who never committed adultery, are now extinct.

—*W. Somerset Maugham (1874–1965)*

85

When I saw my wife in bed with another man, I said, "Get off me, you two."

—*Emo Philips*

86

My father told me that anything worth having is worth waiting for. I waited until I was fifteen.

—*Zsa Zsa Gabor*

87

I'm a nice girl. I hate it on a first date when I accidentally have sex.

—*Emmy Gay*

88

My wife is a sex object. When I ask for sex, she objects.

—*Les Dawson*

89

In ancient times, men sacrificed virgins to the gods. They were careful not to sacrifice sluts.

—*Bill Maher*

90

My wife calls our water bed the Dead Sea.

—*Henry "Henny" Youngman (1906–1998)*

91

It is better to have loved and lost than to have paid for it and not liked it.

—*Hiram Kasten*

92

Mistresses and wives are as different as night and day.

—Abigail Van Buren

93

I tried phone sex and it gave me an ear infection.

—Richard Lewis

94

A lad with his first cigar makes himself sick. A lad with his first girl makes other people sick.

—Mary Wilson Little

95

You know that look women get when they want sex? Me neither.

—*Drew Carey*

96

What do you mean, "Not tonight, I have a headache"? You're a prostitute.

—*Cartoon caption by Robert Mankoff*

97

I'm so afraid of intimacy I learned ventriloquism so I could throw my orgasm.

—*Richard Lewis*

98

I was pretty old before I had my first sexual experience. The reason was that I was born by cesarian section and had no frame of reference.

—*Jeff Hilton*

99

When I go into a bar, I'm not looking for a woman who knows the capital of Maine.

—*David Brenner*

100

I practice safe sex. I use an air bag.

—*Garry Shandling*

101

Safe sex is very important, which is why I'll never do it again on plywood scaffolding.

—*Jenny Jones*

102

I hate safe sex because I can't stand the smell of burning rubber.

—*Strange de Jim*

103

There is no such thing as safe sex and there never will be.

—*Norman Mailer (1923–2007)*

104

I like my sex the way I play basketball. One-on-one with as little dribbling as possible.

—*Leslie Nielsen (1926–2010)*

105

The sheet on his bed crawled around on its own looking for an ovum.

—Jennifer Saunders

106

My live-in boyfriend and I never have sex. Now that the milk is free, we've both become lactose intolerant.

—Margaret Cho

107

Three sex tips for men: slow down, turn off the TV, and call out the right name.

—Jay Leno

108

Coito, *ergo sum.*

—Randall Garrett (1927–1987)

109

A little coitus
Never hoitus.

—Unknown

110

When I was a kid I once stole a pornographic book in braille and rubbed the dirty parts.

—*Woody Allen*

111

In my sex fantasies, nobody ever loves me for my mind.

—*Nora Ephron*

112

I have a tremendous sex drive. My boyfriend lives forty miles away.

—*Phyllis Diller*

113

I slept with a French girl once. It wasn't magical, it wasn't mystical, and it wasn't worth five bucks.

—*Tony Morewood*

114

I once made love to a female clown. She twisted my penis into a poodle.

—*Larry the Cable Guy (Daniel Lawrence Whitney)*

115

Sex change operations are rarely from women to men. That would be a demotion.

—*Ruby Glouster*

116

When the sun comes up, I have morals again.

—*Elayne Boosler*

117

As I grow older and older and totter toward the tomb
I find that I care less and less who goes to bed with
whom.

—*Dorothy Sayers (1893–1957)*

118

My wife uses me. Last night she used me to time an egg.

—*Rodney Dangerfield (1921–2004)*

119

Why do they put Bibles in bedrooms, where it's usually too late?

—*Christopher Morley (1890–1957)*

120

I remember the first time I had sex. I still have the receipt.

—*Groucho Marx (1890–1977)*

121

Never trust a husband too far or a bachelor too near.

—*Helen Rowland (1875–1950)*

122

Puritans should wear fig leaves on their eyes.

—*Stanislaw J. Lec (1909–1966)*

123

Sexual congress in a Mailer novel is always a matter of strenuous activity, rather like mountain climbing.

—*Kate Millet*

124

I'm not your type. My breasts are real.

—*Janeane Garofalo*

125

My girlfriend was famous for her big boobs. I was one of a long line of big boobs that she had.

—Dana Snow

126

The sexual revolution is over and the microbes won.

—P. J. O'Rourke

127

God gave men a penis and a brain, but only enough blood to run one at a time.

—Robin Williams

128

I had sex for five hours once, but four were for apologizing.

—Conan O'Brien

129

Sex is not a crime. It's an expression of love between two or three consenting adults.

—Jeffrey Tambor

130

I'm great in bed. I never fall out.

—Garry Shandling

131

Celibacy is the worst form of self-abuse.

—Peter De Vries (1910–1993)

132

Celibacy is measured in hours.

—Edward Hurst

133

You don't have to be in the KKK to be a wizard under the sheets.

—Unknown

134

A four-hundred-foot diaphragm! Birth control for the whole country!

—Woody Allen

135

When my mom found my diaphragm, I told her it was a bathing cap for my cat.

—*Liz Winston*

136

I rely on my personality for birth control.

—*Liz Winston*

137

For a single woman, the best contraceptive is to yell, "Yes, I want to have your baby!"

—*Marsha Doble*

138

My girlfriend laughs during sex no matter what she's reading.

—*Emo Philips*

139

I'm a heroine addict. I need to have sex with women who have saved someone's life.

—*Mitch Hedberg (1968–2005)*

140

Sometimes I look at a cute guy and get a uterus twinge.

—*Carrie Snow*

141

A hooker told me she'd do anything I wanted for fifty bucks. I said, "Paint my house."

—*Henry "Henny" Youngman (1906–1998)*

142

Today when you get the clap, it's a relief.

—*Brad Garrett*

143

I finally found my wife's G-spot. A neighbor lady had it.

—*Jim Sherbert*

144

I'm against one-night stands. I believe you should get to know someone and be in love with them before you use and degrade them.

—*Steve Person*

145

I married a German. Every night I dressed up as Poland and he invaded me.

—*Bette Midler*

146

The command "Be fruitful and multiply" was issued when the population of the world was two.

—*Dean Inge (1860–1954)*

147

King Solomon said to his thousand wives, "Who hasn't got a headache?"

—*Red Buttons (1919–2006)*

148

When the authorities warn you about the dangers of sex, the lesson is clear: don't have sex with the authorities.

—*Matt Groening*

149

Pizza is like sex. Even when it's bad, you still have to pay for it.

—*Nick Di Paolo*

150

When a man talks dirty to a woman, it's sexual harassment. When a woman talks dirty to a man, it's $4.95 a minute.

—*Jim Shock*

151

There are three words you don't want to hear during sex: "Honey, I'm home . . ."

—*Ken Hammond*

152

Masturbation is the thinking man's television.

—*Christopher Hampton*

153

Intercourse counterfeits masturbation.

—*Jean-Paul Sartre (1905–1980)*

154

When my father told me that masturbation causes blindness, I said, "I'm over here, Dad."

—*Dick Capri*

155

Adolescent boys often find themselves irresistible.

—*Frank McCourt (1930–2009)*

156

In bed, I let the woman come to me. Frankly, I don't even need the woman.

—Garry Shandling

157

Most of the trouble I've gotten into in my life wouldn't have happened if I had masturbated first.

—Roger Nygard

158

I don't play with myself. I was cleaning it once and it went off.

—Larry the Cable Guy (Daniel Lawrence Whitney)

159

Masturbation is shaking hands with the unemployed.

—George Carlin (1937–2008)

160

Explicit love scenes are a turnoff, unless you can read them with one hand.

—Colleen McCullough

161

Who came up with the word *mammogram*? When I hear it, I think I'm supposed to put a breast in an envelope and mail it to somebody.

—Jan King

162

I belong to a group called Sex Without Partners.

—Garry Shandling

163

The biggest, strongest, most powerful men can be reduced by sex to imps.

—Isaac Bashevis Singer (1904–1991)

164

A nymphomaniac is a woman as obsessed with sex as the average man.

—Mignon McLaughlin (1913–1983)

165

We think about sex obsessively except during the act, when our minds tend to wander.

—Howard Nemerov (1920–1991)

166

If you can't stand the heat, stay out of the bedroom.

—David E. Ortman

167

I'm going to the backseat of the car with the woman I love and I won't be back for ten minutes.

—Matt Groening

168

Yuppies have a low birthrate because they have to go to Aspen to mate.

—Dave Barry

169

A woman phoned the other night and said, "Come on over, nobody's home." I went over. Nobody was home.

—Rodney Dangerfield (1921–2004)

170

Many women have trouble looking into a man's eyes because her eyes aren't located in her chest.

—Unknown

171

Incest is relatively boring.

—Unknown

172

I'm so Southern I'm related to myself.

—Brett Butler

173

Being a sex symbol was rather like being a convict.

—*Raquel Welch*

174

Sometimes I shave one leg so it's like going to bed with a woman.

—*Garry Shandling*

175

I once was involved with a woman who was having affairs with eleven other guys. It was a love dodecahedron.

—*Dana Snow*

176

The average cost of one Viagra pill is about $90, given the cost of the drinks and the room.

—*Argus Hamilton*

177

The idea of using Viagra at my age is like erecting a new flagpole in front of a condemned building.

—*Harvey Korman (1927–2008) at age seventy*

178

Virginity is like a balloon: one prick and it's gone.

—Unknown

179

Anybody who listens to my phone messages will find out that I'm pro-choice, pro–animal rights, and a slut.

—Cynthia Heimel

180

I'm not straight and I'm not gay. I'm just a slut. Where is my parade? What about slut pride?

—Margaret Cho

181

It takes a lot of experience to learn how to kiss like a beginner.

—Unknown

182

Chastity is its own punishment.

—James H. Pou Bailey

183

Italian men are so macho they need two or three vasectomies.

—*Garry Shandling*

184

When she saw the MEMBERS ONLY sign she thought of him.

—*Spike Milligan (1918–2002)*

185

God is in my head, but the devil is in my pants.

—*Jonathan Winters*

186

What the world needs is fewer people making more people.

—*George Burns (1896–1996)*

187

To have hot sex you have to tell your partner what you want. How do you tell somebody that you want somebody else?

—*Elayne Boosler*

188

We all worry about the population explosion, but not at the right time.

—*Arthur Hoppe (1925–2000)*

189

What will people be saying about me in a hundred years? "And he's still sexually active!"

—*Bill Bryson*

190

We used to laugh at Grandpa when he'd head off in the morning to go fishing. But we wouldn't laugh in the evening when he'd come back with some whore he'd picked up.

—*Jack Handey*

191

The man who waits for the woman to make the first move is the man of his dreams.

—*Leo Roberts*

192

I hired a prostitute, but all I could afford was a hug, which she called "an arm job."

—Dana Snow

193

My girlfriend wanted to make love in front of a mirror, which meant I had to hold her above the dashboard.

—John Kerwin

194

Nothing is potent against love except impotence.

—Samuel Butler (1835–1902)

195

My wife likes to talk during sex. Last night she called me from a hotel.

—Rodney Dangerfield (1921–2004)

196

Men want a woman they can turn off and on like a light switch.

—Ian Fleming (1908–1964)

197

Do missionaries just call it "the position"?

—Robert Brenneman

198

There's a fine line between eroticism and nausea.

—Sandra Bernhard

199

I asked my wife to rate me as a lover on a scale of one to ten. She said, "You know I'm no good at fractions."

—Rodney Dangerfield (1921–2004)

200

I feel like a million tonight . . . but one at a time.

—Bette Midler

201

I regret to say that the FBI is powerless to act in cases of oral-genital intimacy unless it in some way obstructs interstate commerce.

—J. Edgar Hoover (1895–1972)

202

An orgasm is a population explosion.

—*Chet Hurley*

203

A pirate's climax is an arrgghasm.

—*Leo Roberts*

204

Latin scholars know that the words *penis* and *pencil* are related. Especially in my case.

—*John Kerwin*

205

Nice guys finish last.

—*Charlie Caruso*

206

At the request of the Catholic Church, a three-day sex orgy this weekend was canceled, so I stayed home and cleaned my house.

—*Tina Fey*

207

Don't bother discussing sex with small children. They rarely have anything to add.

—Fran Lebowitz

208

Nun. The word says it all.

—Rue McClanahan (1934–2010) on The Golden Girls

209

Sex is like art. Most of it is pretty bad and the good stuff is out of your price range.

—Scott Roeben

210

I'm such a terrible lover I've actually given a woman an anticlimax.

—Scott Roeben

211

I wasn't naked. I was completely covered by a blue spotlight.

—Stripteaser Gypsy Rose Lee (1914–1970)

212

Women should be obscene and not heard.

—*John Lennon (1940–1980)*

213

When in doubt about yourself or your career, take off your clothes. It has always worked for me.

—*Former stripper Carol Doda*

214

I never made any money until I took off my pants.

—*Burlesque dancer Sally Rand (1904–1979)*

215

The primary function of breasts is to make men stupid.

—*Dave Barry*

216

Pamela Anderson confirmed that she has had her breast implants removed. Doctors say she is doing fine and that her old implants are now dating Charlie Sheen.

—*Conan O'Brien*

217

Sex in New York City is different because it happens in smaller rooms.

—*Sherry Lansing*

218

Sex is like money; only too much is enough.

—*John Updike (1932–2009)*

219

I was on a date with a woman and asked her if she had brought any protection. She pulled a knife.

—*Scott Roeben*

220

The hot pants she was wearing were so tight I could hardly breathe.

—*Benny Hill (1925–1992)*

221

Sex for free usually costs more than sex for money.

—*Brendan Behan (1923–1964)*

222

If God wanted us to have group sex, he would have given us more organs.

—Malcolm Bradbury (1932–2000)

223

If her lips are on fire and she trembles in your arms, she's got malaria.

—Jackie Kannon

224

My girlfriend is the most wonderful person in the world to me. But not to my wife.

—Jackie Mason

225

My grandmother died while having sex. I still cry when I watch the video.

—Larry Reeb

226

I accidentally walked in on my roommate and his girlfriend having sex. They didn't see me for almost ten minutes.

—Nathan Trenholm

227

Never be unfaithful to a lover, except with your wife.

—P. J. O'Rourke

228

Robert Benchley and I shared an office so small that one inch smaller and it would have been adultery.

—Dorothy Parker (1893–1967)

229

When I have a headache at bedtime, my husband hides the aspirin.

—Joan Rivers

230

The pharaoh Ramses II had fifty children. Who decided to name a condom after him?

—Conan O'Brien

231

Don't have sex. It leads to kissing and pretty soon you have to start talking to them.

—Steve Martin

232

Of all the sexual aberrations, chastity is the strangest.

—*Anatole France (1844–1924)*

233

Men want the same thing from their underwear that they want from women: a little bit of support and a little bit of freedom.

—*Jerry Seinfeld*

234

I'm sleeping alone now thanks to the exterminator.

—*Emo Philips*

235

Ducking for apples—change one letter and it's the story of my life.

—*Dorothy Parker (1893–1967)*

236

If I'm not in bed by eleven, I go home.

—*Henny Youngman (1906–1998)*

237

Never do anything to your partner with your teeth that you wouldn't do to an expensive wristwatch.

—*P. J. O'Rourke*

238

Whatever else can be said about sex, it can't be called a dignified performance.

—*Helen Lawrenson (1908–1982)*

239

Homosexuality in Russia is punishable by seven years in prison, confined with other homosexuals. There is a three-year waiting list.

—*Yakov Smirnoff*

240

Martina Navratilova was so far in the closet that she was in danger of becoming a garment bag.

—*Rita Mae Brown*

241

I recently had my first homosexual experience. Two lesbians beat the hell out of me.

—*Dan Bradley*

MEN AND WOMEN

242

I like the concept of "men." It's the reality I have trouble with.

—Stefanie H. Piro

243

You have to be very fond of men to love them. Otherwise they're simply unbearable.

—Marguerite Duras (1914–1996)

244

I tried American girls. They talk too much.

—Manute Bol (1963–2010)

245

Men are not given awards for bravery in intimacy.

—Gail Sheehy

246

There are two reasons why the world is so screwed up: men and women.

—*Unknown*

247

There are two kinds of people. You're not one of them.

—*Cartoon caption by Bruce Erik Kaplan*

248

Men are from Earth, women are from Earth. Deal with it.

—*George Carlin (1937–2008)*

249

Women are from Venus, men are from Sears.

—*Rebecca Christian*

250

Nobody is completely worthless. Some can be used as bad examples.

—*John Tigges (1932–2008)*

251

Until you've lost your reputation, you never realize what a burden it was.

—*Margaret Mitchell (1900–1949)*

252

People with no vices usually have annoying virtues.

—*British novelist Elizabeth Taylor (1912–1975)*

253

Women's virtue is man's greatest invention.

—*Cornelia Otis Skinner (1899–1979)*

254

Good girls go to heaven, bad girls go everywhere.

—*Helen Gurley Brown*

255

When he said we were trying to make a fool of him, I could only murmur that the Creator had beat us to it.

—*Ilka Chase (1900–1978)*

256

Men don't understand pain. They've never experienced labor, cramps, or bikini wax.

—*Nan Tisdale*

257

Men do cry, but only when assembling furniture.

—*Rita Rudner*

258

Some men believe that every woman's secret desire is to have the fine points of football demonstrated with the silverware.

—*Jane Campbell*

259

The male is a domestic animal which, if treated with firmness and kindness, can be trained to do most things.

—*Jilly Cooper*

260

A man is so in the way in a house.

—*Elizabeth Gaskell (1810–1865)*

261

Rubbing elbows with a man will reveal things about him you never before realized. So will rubbing fenders.

—*Thelma Doss (1927–2011)*

262

Never underestimate a man's ability to underestimate a woman's ability.

—*From the movie* V.I. Warshawski, *1991*

263

Friends are not necessarily the people you like best, they are merely the people who got there first.

—*Peter Ustinov (1921–2004)*

264

It's better to be looked over than overlooked.

—*Mae West (1893–1980)*

265

Plain women know more about men than beautiful ones do.

—*Katharine Hepburn (1907–2003)*

266

If a man speaks and there is no woman to hear him, is he still wrong?

—*Unknown*

267

Marge, it's three a.m. Shouldn't you be baking?

—*Homer Simpson (Matt Groening)*

268

People enjoy things more when they know a lot of other people have been left out.

—*Russell Baker*

269

Flattery is so necessary to all of us that we flatter one another just to be flattered in return.

—*Marjorie Bowen (1885–1952)*

270

There's a difference between beauty and charm. A beautiful woman is one I notice. A charming woman is one who notices me.

—*John Erskine (1879–1951)*

271

The difference between government bonds and men is the government bonds mature.

—Debbie Perry

272

A good woman is one of the greatest things on earth, second only perhaps to a good child or a good man.

—Stephen Leacock (1869–1944)

273

A woman should be an illusion.

—Ian Fleming (1908–1964)

274

If a woman hasn't met the right man by the time she is twenty-four, she may be lucky.

—Deborah Kerr (1921–2007)

275

We are so vain we even care for the opinion of those we don't care for.

—Marie von Ebner-Eschenbach (1830–1916)

276

Roosters crow, hens deliver.

—*Feminist slogan*

277

Hang on to the thought that every dog has its day, even the bitches.

—*Colleen McCullough*

278

If women were as big as men, we'd be in real trouble.

—*Terry McDonald*

279

Because men are bigger than us, we learned to be the sneakier of the two sexes.

—*Cher*

280

A man should be taller, older, heavier, hoarser, and uglier than his wife.

—*Edgar Watson Howe (1853–1937)*

281

Men make passes at girls who wear glasses so they can see themselves in the reflection.

—*Stephanie Calman*

282

Unless they are cheating, men buy lousy presents.

—*Cynthia Heimel*

283

Most love triangles are wrecktangles.

—Jacob Braude

284

Send two dozen roses to room 424 and write "I love you, Emily" on the back of the bill.

—Groucho Marx (1890–1977)

285

If a woman's work is never done, she should start earlier.

—Ron Stevens

286

Women and cats will do as they please, and men and dogs should get used to the idea.

—Robert Heinlein (1907–1988)

287

The way to fight a woman is with your hat. Grab it and run.

—John Barrymore (1882–1942)

288

The only place a man can feel really secure is in a maximum-security prison, except for the imminent threat of release.

—Germaine Greer

289

She laughs at everything you say. Why? Because she has fine teeth.

—Benjamin Franklin (1706–1790)

290

One can't be always laughing at a man without now and then stumbling on something witty.

—Jane Austen (1775–1817)

291

When women are depressed they either eat or go shopping. Men invade another country. It's a whole different way of thinking.

—Elayne Boosler

292

Men differ from women. Young men never sit around talking about their dream weddings.

—*Charles Cosart*

293

Women should be called estrogen-Americans.

—*Garrison Keillor*

294

Women speak in estrogen and men listen in testosterone.

—*Matt Groening*

295

The man who won't lie to a woman has very little consideration for her feelings.

—*Bergen Evans (1904–1978)*

296

There are two kinds of people, the prickly and the gooey.

—*Alan Watts (1915–1973)*

297

I'm just a couch potato looking for a couch tomato.

—*Unnamed San Francisco official quoted by Herb Caen (1916–1997)*

298

All men are afraid of eyelash curlers. I keep one under my pillow instead of a gun.

—*Rita Rudner*

299

When the trust goes out of a relationship, it's no fun lying anymore.

—*From the TV series* Cheers

300

People call me a feminist whenever I express sentiments that differentiate me from a doormat.

—*Rebecca West (1892–1983)*

301

I don't put on makeup everyday. I use that time to clean my rifle.

—*Henrietta Mantel*

302

The vote means nothing to women. We should be armed.

—*Edna O'Brien*

303

By the time I'd grown up, I naturally supposed that I'd be grown up.

—*Eve Babitz*

304

The difference between men and women is that a man can walk past a shoe store, especially if he already has a pair of shoes.

—*Gallagher*

305

If men liked shopping, they'd call it research.

—*Cynthia Nelms*

306

How do you know when it's time to wash the dishes and clean the house? If you have a penis, it's not time.

—*Jo Brand*

307

MACHO stands for Men Avoiding Chores at Home and Outside.

—*Ernestine Ulmer*

308

The Englishwoman is so refined
She has no bosom and no behind.

—Stevie Smith (1902–1971)

309

If men menstruated instead of women, religious ceremonies and family dinners would mark the day.

—Gloria Steinem

310

Aristotle could have avoided the mistake of thinking that women have fewer teeth than men by the simple device of asking Mrs. Aristotle to open her mouth.

—Bertrand Russell (1872–1970)

311

Men's underwear should come with expiration dates.

—Diane Ford

312

Women who buy perfume and flowers for themselves because men don't do it are called "self-basting."

—Adair Lara

313

The classic function of the warrior helped men throughout history achieve a sense of confidence they needed in order to cope with women.

—Page Smith (1917–1995)

314

Men in singles bars have one thing in common: they're married.

—Cindy Garner

315

When women came up with PMS, men came up with ESPN.

—Blake Clark

316

There should be PMS shelters for men.

—*Jeff Foxworthy*

317

Men lie so much it's almost a language.

—*Chris Rock*

318

What is my favorite romantic spot? You mean in the whole world or on somebody's body?

—*Jackie Mason*

319

I once wore a peekaboo blouse. People would peek, then they'd boo.

—*Phyllis Diller*

320

I once burned my bra. It took the fire department four days to put it out.

—*Dolly Parton*

321

If you want to say it with flowers, remember that a single rose screams, "I'm cheap."

—Delta Burke, on the TV series Designing Women

322

You can say it with flowers
You can say it with wine;
But if you want to make her stinkin' sentimental,
Say it with a Lincoln Continental.

—Chet Hurley

323

My girlfriend says I never listen to her. I think that's what she said.

—Drake Sather (1959–2004)

324

Never sign a valentine with your own name.

—Charles Dickens (1812–1870)

325

I'm loyal in my relationships. When I go out with my mom, I don't look at other moms.

—Garry Shandling

326

Being at a loss for words has saved many relationships.

—Bill Watterson

327

My troubles don't come from chasing women. They begin when I catch them.

—John Barrymore (1882–1942)

328

I finally found the perfect woman. Unfortunately, she was looking for the perfect man.

—Unknown

329

She had the Midas touch. Everything she touched turned into a muffler.

—Lisa Smerling

330

A woman need know but one man well to understand all men; whereas a man may know all women and understand not one of them.

—Helen Rowland (1876–1950)

331

Men put women on a pedestal so they won't have to look them in the eye.

—Marian Stewart

332

Women must come down off the pedestal. Men put us there to get us out of the way.

—Sybil Thomas (Lady Rhonda, 1857–1941)

333

Now that I'm financially successful, my shopping blunders are bigger.

—Cathy Guisewite

334

Women are crazy and men are stupid. The reason women are crazy is that men are stupid.

—George Carlin (1937–2008)

335

As long as the world is turning, we're going to be dizzy and make mistakes.

—Mel Brooks

336

It's hard to feel morally superior to a person who gets up earlier than you do.

—*Mary Gordon*

337

All men are frauds. The only difference between them is that some admit it. I myself deny it.

—*H. L. Mencken (1880–1956)*

338

When somebody says, "The last thing I want to do is hurt you," it means they have other things to do first.

—*Mark Schiff*

MEN AND MEN

339

I knocked on the door of a toilet stall to see if it was occupied and a voice said, "Come in."

—Ron Richards

340

I was thrown out of the army for contributing to the delinquency of a major.

—Strange de Jim

341

Trinity Episcopal in San Francisco is a "gay nineties" church. Everybody is either gay or ninety.

—Robert Cromey, rector (retired)

342

You're a transvestite, aren't you? I like that in a man.

—Cartoon caption by John Callahan (1951–2010)

343

The purpose of women in American movies is to prove that the male protagonist is not gay.

—Film director Pedro Almodóvar

344

If Michelangelo had been straight, the Sistine Chapel would have been wallpapered.

—Robin Tyler

345

If Michelangelo had been straight, the Sistine Chapel would have been painted basic white with a roller.

—Rita Mae Brown

346

There is nothing wrong with being gay. I have plenty of friends who are going to hell.

—Stephen Colbert

347

Every straight man should be locked in a closet with a gay man until he learns how to dress.

—Judy Tenuta

348

My brother is gay, but my parents don't care as long as he marries a doctor.

—Elayne Boosler

349

If homosexuality is inherited, shouldn't it have died out by now?

—George Booth

350

Miller Beer is running openly gay ads. The guys are using coasters.

—*Craig Kilborn*

351

I was born gay, but eight months of breast feeding turned me straight.

—*Nick Di Paolo*

352

I don't remember if my first sexual experience was with a man or woman. I was too polite to ask.

—*Gore Vidal*

LOVE

353

Love is the only disease that makes you feel better.

—Sam Shepard

354

Love is a disease, but curable.

—Dame Rose Macaulay (1881–1958)

355

Love is an agreement on the part of two people to overestimate each other.

—E. M. Cioran (1911–1995)

356

No one ever died of love, so you're going to need a gun.

—From the Onion, *December 7, 2000*

357

Love is a slippery eel that bites like hell.

—Bertrand Russell (1872–1970)

358

Scratch a lover, find a foe.

—Dorothy Parker (1893–1967)

359

A strong pair of glasses is sometimes enough to cure a person in love.

—Friedrich Nietzsche (1844–1900)

360

If love is the answer, could you rephrase the question?

—Lily Tomlin

361

Love, like restaurant hash, must be taken with blind faith or it loses its flavor.

—Helen Rowland (1876–1950)

362

To fall in love, you have to be in the state of mind for it to take, like a disease.

—*Nancy Mitford (1904–1973)*

363

We tend not to believe in love or rheumatism until after the first attack.

—*Marie von Ebner-Eschenbach (1830–1916)*

364

The great thing about unrequited love is that it's the only kind that lasts.

—*Allison Pearson*

365

I'd rather be in jail than in love again.

—*Peter Chelsom*

366

Love! The walks over soft grass, the smiles over candle-light, the arguments over everything else.

—*From the TV show* Max Headroom, *1987*

367

The one who loves the least controls the relationship.

—*Robert Anthony*

368

I fall in love with any girl who smells of library paste.

—*Charlie Brown (Charles Schulz, 1922–2000)*

369

Love is staying up all night with a sick child or a healthy adult.

—*David Frost*

370

L-O-V-E spells *love*, but so does C-A-S-H.

—*Johnny Carson (1925–2005)*

371

No matter how lovesick a woman is, she shouldn't take the first pill who comes along.

—*Dr. Joyce Brothers*

372

Love is like the measles—all the worse when it comes late in life.

—Douglas Jerrold (1803–1857)

373

Sometimes I need what only you can provide—your absence.

—Ashleigh Brilliant

374

Before I met my husband, I'd never fallen in love, though I'd stepped in it a few times.

—Rita Rudner

375

Falling out of love is very enlightening. For a short while you see the world with new eyes.

—Iris Murdoch (1919–1999)

376

Platonic love is being invited into the wine cellar for a sip of pop.

—Unknown

377

Nobody loves me like my mother, and she could be jivin'.

—*B.B. King*

378

How do I love thee? Sometimes I wonder.

—*Unknown*

379

"I love you," he said, with his tongue in her cheek.

—*Sydney Hoddes*

380

Men look at love the same way they look at smoke from their car engines: "Damn, how much is this going to cost me?"

—*Tim Conlon*

381

Religion has done love a great service by making it a sin.

—*Anatole France (1844–1924)*

382

The man with lots of friends who slaps everybody on the back is regarded as having no friends.

—Aristotle (384–322 BC)

383

Love your enemy—it will drive him nuts.

—Eleanor Doan

384

Only time can heal a broken heart, just as only time can heal his broken arms and legs.

—Miss Piggy (Henry Beard)

385

If I'm lucky, I'll fall in love. If I'm unlucky, I'll fall and hit my head.

—Emmy Gay

386

Grumbling is the death of love.

—*Marlene Dietrich (1901–1992)*

387

Fond as we are of our loved ones, there comes at times during their absence an unexplained peace.

—*Anne Shaw*

MARRIAGE

388

A paddle-wheel riverboat is as beautiful as a wedding cake, without the complications.

—*Mark Twain (1835–1910)*

389

I want a big church wedding and he wants to break off the engagement.

—*Sally Poplin*

390

At weddings, one family is always better than the other.

—*Jeff Foxworthy*

391

There's always one teacher you have a crush on. For me it's my wife's aerobics instructor.

—*Brian Kiley*

392

When you first buy a house, you notice the pretty paint. The second time you check the basement for termites. It's the same with marriage.

—*Lupe Valdez*

393

Why dust the house when you can just wait a couple of years and get a snowblower?

—*Roseanne Barr*

394

One of the pleasures of being messy is that you are always making exciting discoveries.

—Unknown

395

Housework can't kill you, but why take a chance?

—Phyllis Diller

396

Since I have become nearsighted, I can't see dust or squalor and conceive of myself as living in splendor.

—Alice James (1848–1892)

397

Tom Arnold and I didn't sign a prenuptial agreement. We signed a mutual suicide pact.

—Roseanne Barr

398

Marrying a man is like buying something you've been admiring for a long time. It doesn't always go with everything else in the house.

—Jean Kerr (1922–2003)

399

Sometimes you have to know somebody really well to discover that you're really strangers.

—Mary Tyler Moore

400

I want a husband who is kind and understanding. Is that too much to ask of a multimillionaire?

—Zsa Zsa Gabor

401

If it weren't for marriage, men would spend their lives thinking they had no faults at all.

—Unknown

402

I married a woman who had no interest in me because that's the only kind I knew.

—Ed Wedge

403

If you can't remember the last time you had sex with a woman, you're either gay or married.

—Jeff Foxworthy

404

My husband and I have a really good system for housework. Neither one of us does it.

—Dottie Archibald

405

Honeymoon lunch: lettuce alone without dressing.

—Susan Richman

406

The trouble with marrying for money is that you end up earning it.

—Lauren Bacall

407

My lesbianism is an act of Christian charity. All those women out there praying for a man can have my share.

—Rita Mae Brown

408

I'm too interested in other men's wives to think of getting one of my own.

—George Moore (1852–1933)

409

There's nothing like a good dose of another woman to make a man appreciate his wife.

—*Clare Boothe Luce (1903–1987)*

410

If you marry or if you don't marry, you will regret it.

—*Soren Kierkegaard (1813–1855)*

411

Marriage is an adventure, like going to war.

—*G. K. Chesterton (1874–1936)*

412

Get married. If you have a good wife, you'll be happy; if not, you'll become a philosopher.

—*Socrates (470–399 BC)*

413

I married my wife for her looks, but not the kind she's giving me lately.

—*Jeff Foxworthy*

414

Politics doesn't make strange bedfellows, marriage does.

—Groucho Marx (1890–1977)

415

Getting married for sex is like buying a 747 for the peanuts.

—Jeff Foxworthy

416

If love means never having to say you're sorry, then marriage means having to say everything twice.

—Estelle Getty (1923–2008)

417

All marriages are mixed marriages.

—Chantal Saperstein

418

Marriage: from Niagara to Viagra.

—Paul Hemmer

419

It should be a happy marriage—they are both so much in love with him.

—Irene Thomas (1919–2001)

420

Marriage is tough because you have to deal with feelings and lawyers.

—Richard Pryor (1940–2005)

421

My wife doesn't. Understand me?

—William Cole (1912–1992)

422

I asked my husband if he wanted to renew our marriage vows. He got all excited because he thought they had expired.

—Rita Rudner

423

Frank and I used to work at our marriage. Now we're retired.

—Cartoon caption by Ed Arno (1916–2008)

424

When he is late for dinner and I know that he is either having an affair or lying dead in the street, I always hope he's dead.

—*Judith Viorst*

425

If you can't have your husband as a comfort and delight, use him as a cross to bear.

—*Stevie Smith (1902–1971)*

426

A woman who takes her husband about with her everywhere is like a cat playing with a mouse long after she's killed it.

—*Saki (H. H. Munro, 1870–1916)*

427

I love being married. When I was single, I got so sick of finishing my own sentences.

—*Brian Kiley*

428

Don't forget Mother's Day, which in Beverly Hills is called Dad's Third Wife Day.

—Jay Leno

429

Marriage requires commitment. So does insanity.

—Groucho Marx (1890–1977)

430

I could marry anybody I pleased. So far, I haven't pleased anybody.

—Ruth Buzzi

431

Bigamy is having one wife too many. So is monogamy.

—Erica Jong

432

My wife and I took out insurance policies on each other, so now it's just a waiting game.

—Bill Dwyer

433

I had a few words for my wife, and she had a few paragraphs for me.

—*Thomas Gifford (1937–2000)*

434

If marriage is the most natural state, how come married people always look nauseous?

—*Jackie Mason*

435

If variety is the spice of life, marriage is the big can of leftover SPAM.

—*Johnny Carson (1925–2005)*

436

When you see a married couple walking down the street, the one that's a few steps ahead is the one that's mad.

—*Daniel Tosh*

437

Marriage is nature's way of keeping us from fighting with strangers.

—*Alan King (1927–2004)*

438

For two people to be able to live together for the rest of their lives is almost unnatural.

—Jane Fonda

439

There is almost no marital problem that can't be helped by taking off your clothes.

—Garrison Keillor

440

A wholesome sexual relationship changes with marriage because all of a sudden you're sleeping with a relative.

—Andrew Ward

441

In love with her own husband? Monstrous! What a selfish woman!

—Jennie Jerome Churchill (1854–1921)

442

Love: the quest. Marriage: the conquest. Divorce: the inquest.

—Helen Rowland (1876–1950)

443

Before marriage, a man will lay down his life for you; after marriage he won't even lay down his newspaper.

—Helen Rowland (1876–1950)

444

Married men live longer than single men, but they suffer a slow, torturous death.

—*Larry Reeb*

445

Eighty is the best age for getting married because then you can be sure it will last.

—*Lauren Bacall*

446

Marriage is a competition in suffering.

—*Arthur Hoppe (1925–2000)*

447

If you really loved me, you would have married somebody else.

—*Bill Hoest,* The Lockhorns *(1926–1988)*

448

When you marry your mistress, you create a job vacancy.

—*James Goldsmith*

449

A fool and his money are soon married.

—*Variously ascribed*

450

Being married reduces the chance of a heart attack or anything exciting.

—*Jonathan Katz*

451

Every man wants a woman to appeal to his better side, his nobler instincts, and his higher nature—and another woman to help him forget them.

—*Helen Rowland (1876–1950)*

452

It's very hard to live in the same house with someone all the time if you are a grown-up person.

—Katharine Hepburn (1907–2003)

453

Married couples should be separated at dinner parties so that each one can tell stories without contradiction.

—Miss Manners (Judith Martin)

454

In some countries, marriage is used as a punishment for shoplifting.

—From the movie Wayne's World, *1992*

455

Just because I have rice on my clothes doesn't mean I've been to a wedding. A Chinese man threw up on me.

—Phyllis Diller

456

Being married means always having someone to blame.

—Cynthia Louise Laffoon

457

It is always incomprehensible to a man that a woman should ever refuse an offer of marriage.

—Jane Austen (1775–1817)

458

I'm going to get married again because I'm more mature now and I need some kitchen stuff.

—Wendy Liebman

459

All marriages are happy. It's trying to live together afterward that causes the problems.

—Shelley Winters (1920–2006)

460

Whenever I get married, I start buying *Gourmet* magazine.

—Nora Ephron

461

I always know when my mother-in-law is coming because the mice start throwing themselves on the traps.

—Les Dawson

462

Because I love my house, I will not cheat on my wife.

—*Chas Elstner*

463

The critical time in a marriage is breakfast.

—*A. P. Herbert (1890–1971)*

464

My wife doesn't like to see me in pain unless she is inflicting it.

—*Buck Rogers*

465

One of the oldest human needs is to have someone to wonder where you are if you don't come home at night.

—*Margaret Mead (1901–1978)*

466

Sleeping alone is better than sleeping alone together.

—*Unknown*

467

It isn't premarital sex if you have no intention of getting married.

—*Matt Barry*

468

If you hate solitude, avoid marriage.

—*Anton Chekhov (1860–1904)*

469

After twenty-seven years of marriage, my wife and I have achieved sexual compatibility. Now we get simultaneous headaches.

—*Clifford Kuhn*

470

My marriage is childless, except for my husband.

—*Cindy Garner*

471

I was married for two years, which is a long time if you divide it into half-hour segments.

—*Charisse Savarin*

472

I had five years of happy marriage, which is not bad out of fifteen.

—*Bob Thomas*

473

Most men who are not married by the age of thirty-five are either homosexual or smart.

—*Becky Rodenbeck*

474

If your husband snores, try sleeping in separate towns.

—*Katharine Whitehorn*

475

A bachelor is like a good detergent: works fast and leaves no ring.

—*Terry Caterbury*

476

Both of my ex-wives closed their eyes when making love because they didn't want to see me having a good time.

—*Joseph Wambaugh*

477

Your spouse should be just attractive enough to turn you on. Anything more is trouble.

—*Albert Brooks*

478

The secret of success is a good wife and a steady job, my wife told me.

—*Howard Nemerov (1920–1991)*

479

Playboy is coming out with an edition for married men. Every month the same centerfold.

—*Craig Kilborn*

480

When we first met, my wife didn't like me. Fortunately, she wanted to stay in this country.

—*Brian Kiley*

481

Marriage is the only adventure open to the cowardly.

—*Voltaire (1694–1778)*

482

I told my mother-in-law that my house was her house, and she said, "Get the hell off my property."

—*Joan Rivers*

483

Attila the Hun decided to get married again because he had been terribly misunderstood the first three hundred times.

—*Will Cuppy (1884–1949)*

484

Marriage starts with passion and ends with laundry.

—*Thomas J. Hogan*

485

If you want your wife to listen to every word you say, talk in your sleep.

—*Unknown*

486

I never got married because I couldn't see bringing a partner in for my money.

—*Jackie Mason, who got married in 1991 at the age of fifty-five*

487

Marriage is a souvenir of love.

—*Helen Rowland (1876–1950)*

488

A man is as faithful as his options.

—*Bill Maher*

489

Caesar might have married Cleopatra, but he had a wife at home. There's always something.

—*Will Cuppy (1884–1949)*

490

The nation should return to colonial values, when a wife was judged by the amount of wood she could split.

—*W. C. Fields (1880–1946)*

491

How many husbands have I had? You mean apart from my own?

—*Zsa Zsa Gabor*

492

My mother buried three husbands, and two of them were just napping.

—*Rita Rudner*

493

A man in Utah is in trouble for having five wives. That's what happens in a society without alcohol, tobacco, or porn.

—*Jon Stewart*

494

The penalty for six wives is six mothers-in-law.

—*Jay Leno*

495

A wedding is like a funeral except that you get to smell your own flowers.

—*Grace Hansen*

496

Never marry a man who refers to the rehearsal dinner as the Last Supper.

—*Unknown*

497

The ideal husband is one who treats his wife like a new car.

—*Dan Bennett*

498

Half of all marriages end in divorce, half in death. You could be one of the lucky ones.

—*Richard Jeni (1957–2007)*

499

Many a good hanging prevents a bad marriage.

—*William Shakespeare (1564–1616)*

500

I watch the videotape of my wedding backwards for the happy ending where I'm backing out of the church.

—Louis Johnson

501

Never marry for money. Divorce for money.

—Wendy Liebman

502

If a couple from the Ozarks moves to California and gets a divorce, are they still legally brother and sister?

—"Super" Dave Osborne (Bob Einstein)

503

Marriage is a mistake every man should make.

—George Jessel (1898–1981)

504

Never ask your wife if she still hears from her old pimp.

—Johnny Carson (1925–2005)

505

Not all women give most of their waking hours to pleasing men. Some are married.

—*Emma Lee*

506

The older men get, the younger their new wives get.

—*Elizabeth Taylor (1932–2011)*

507

I am a very committed wife . . . and I should be committed for being married so many times.

—*Elizabeth Taylor (1932–2011)*

508

It destroys one's nerves to be amiable every day to the same human being.

—Benjamin Disraeli (1804–1881)

509

Perhaps men and women should live next door to each other and just visit now and then.

—Katharine Hepburn (1907–2003)

510

Being an old maid is like death by drowning, a really delightful sensation after you cease to struggle.

—Edna Ferber (1887–1968)

511

A woman who can't forgive should never have more than a nodding acquaintance with a man.

—Edgar Watson Howe (1853–1937)

512

How to Be Happy Though Married

—Book title by E. J. Hardy (1849–1920)

513

Wife to husband: "It isn't the snoring I mind—it's the talking noise you make during the day."

—*Cartoon caption by Michael Maslin*

514

A young person who either marries or dies is sure to be well spoken of.

—*Jane Austen (1775–1817)*

515

My dad has been married so many times that if wives were sandwiches, the next one would be free.

—*Jimmy Pardo*

516

Studies show that only 25 percent of husbands kiss their wife good-bye when they leave the house. However, 99 percent kiss their house good-bye when they leave their wife.

—*Kevin Nealon*

517

Marriage is not just spiritual communion, it is also remembering to take out the trash.

—Dr. Joyce Brothers

518

When a husband's story is believed, he begins to suspect his wife.

—H. L. Mencken (1880–1956)

519

All work and no play makes a housewife.

—Evan Esar (1899–1995)

520

When I finally met Mr. Right, I didn't know his first name was Always.

—Rita Rudner

521

A bachelor is a fellow who never makes the same mistake once.

—From the movie North West Mounted Police, *1940*

BIRTHING AND BABIES

522

Giving birth is like pushing a flaming log through your nostril.

—Unknown

523

Giving birth is like taking your lower lip and forcing it over your head.

—Carol Burnett

524

Watching a baby being born is like watching a wet Saint Bernard squeezing through the cat door.

—Jeff Foxworthy

525

A baby is an alimentary canal with a loud voice at one end and no responsibility at the other.

—Elizabeth Adamson (1883–1965)

526

Giving birth underwater may be less traumatic for the baby, but it's more traumatic for the other people in the pool.

—Elayne Boosler

527

I'll never have a baby because I'm afraid I'll leave it on top of the car.

—Liz Winston

528

If you drive, don't park. Accidents cause people.

—Unknown

529

It serves me right for putting all my eggs in one bastard.

—A pregnant Dorothy Parker (1893–1967) on her way to the hospital

530

I was so ugly when I was born the doctor slapped everybody.

—Jim Bailey as Phyllis Diller

531

My wife was in labor for thirty-two hours and I was faithful to her the whole time.

—Jonathan Katz

532

Pregnancy is amazing! To think that you can create a human being just with things you have around the house!

—Amy Foster

533

The bride was six months pregnant, so we threw puffed rice.

—From The Dick Cavett Show

534

We'd need less gun control if we had better birth control.

—Richard Jeni (1957–2007)

535

My best birth control now is to leave the lights on.

—Joan Rivers

536

My wife's gotten very lazy, or, as she calls it, pregnant.

—*Unknown*

537

In the maternity ward, a wedding ring is a status symbol.

—*Erma Bombeck (1927–1996)*

538

Babies are nauseated by the smell of a clean shirt.

—*Jeff Foxworthy*

539

Why name your baby Arthur? Every Tom, Dick, and Harry is named Arthur.

—Samuel Goldwyn (1882–1974)

540

Why would a forty-nine-year-old woman want to have a baby? So they can both be in diapers at the same time?

—Sue Kolinsky

541

Unfortunately, Joan Collins can't be with us tonight. She is attending the birth of her next husband.

—John Parrott

542

If pregnancy were a book, they'd cut the last two chapters.

—Nora Ephron

543

A Harvard Medical School study has determined that rectal thermometers are still the best way to take a baby's temperature. Plus, it teaches the baby who's boss.

—Tina Fey

544

A couple in California tried to sell their baby for $29 in a Wal-Mart parking lot. Wal-Mart cited the incident as proof of its unbeatable low prices.

—Jimmy Fallon

545

Babies have big heads and big eyes and tiny little bodies with tiny arms and legs. So did the aliens at Roswell. I rest my case.

—William Shatner

546

Never change diapers in midstream.

—Don Marquis (1878–1937)

547

A man finds out what is meant by a spitting image when he tries to feed cereal to his infant.

—Imogene Fey

548

When I was born, my father spent three weeks looking for a loophole in my birth certificate.

—Jackie Vernon (1924–1987)

549

There are two things in life for which we are never truly prepared: twins.

—Josh Billings (1818–1885)

550

Whenever I go to a family reunion, I feel like having my tubes tied.

—Cathy Ladman

551

Families with babies and families without babies are sorry for each other.

—*Edgar Watson Howe (1853–1937)*

552

Thinking that having another baby will save your marriage is like thinking another iceberg would have saved the *Titanic.*

—*Chet Hurley*

553

Cleanliness is next to godliness, which is why I baptized my kids in Pine-Sol.

—*Stephen Colbert*

554

I was born because my mother needed a fourth at meals.

—*Beatrice Lillie (1894–1989)*

CHILDREN

555

Children are little people who don't pay rent.

—*Rick Reynolds*

556

Everything else you grow out of, but you never recover from childhood.

—*Beryl Bainbridge (1932–2010)*

557

I have a love child who sends me hate mail.

—*George Carlin (1937–2008)*

558

There is this to be said about children: they keep you feeling old.

—*Jean Kerr (1922–2003)*

559

I have no children. I don't take hostages.

—*Penny Arcade*

560

Children know that parents, because of their size, are difficult to discipline properly.

—*P. J. O'Rourke*

561

Having a two-year-old is like having a blender with no lid.

—*Jerry Seinfeld*

562

There are trial marriages, but there is no such thing as a trial child.

—Gail Sheehy

563

The imaginary friends I had as a kid dropped me because their friends thought I didn't exist.

—Aaron Machado

564

Before I had kids, I went home after work to rest. Now I go to work to rest.

—Simon Ruddell

565

Children are all foreigners.

—Ralph Waldo Emerson (1803–1882)

566

Adopt a child. Avoid stretch marks.

—Turi Ryder

567

Childhood is a disease you grow out of.

—*William Golding (1911–1993)*

568

When you are eight years old, nothing is your business.

—*Lenny Bruce (1925–1966)*

569

The secret of eternal youth is arrested development.

—*Alice Roosevelt Longworth (1884–1980)*

570

There is nothing so aggravating as a boy who is too old to ignore and too young to kick.

—*Elbert Hubbard (1856–1915)*

571

Youth is a disease that must be borne patiently. Time will cure it.

—*R. H. Benson (1871–1914)*

572

If there were no schools to take children part of the time, insane asylums would be filled with mothers.

—*Edgar Watson Howe (1853–1937)*

573

If your parents never had children, chances are you won't either.

—Dick Cavett

574

I'm going to clean up this dump as soon as the kids are grown.

—Erma Bombeck (1927–1996)

575

Successful parents have adult children who can pay for their own psychoanalysis.

—Nora Ephron

576

My mother told me, "If a strange man ever asks you to get in his car, get in."

—Woody Allen

577

As soon as I stepped out of my mother's womb onto dry land, I realized that I had made a mistake and shouldn't have come. But the trouble with children is that they are not returnable.

—Quentin Crisp (1908–1999)

578

My father had a profound influence on me. He was a lunatic.

—Spike Milligan (1918–2002)

579

My wife wanted to call our daughter Sue, but I felt that in our family that was usually a verb.

—Dennis Wolfberg (1946–1994)

580

My parents named me Zbigniew because they were drunk.

—Cartoon caption by Robert Wagner

581

My father wrote the book on child development. Unfortunately, he wrote it in Norwegian.

—From the movie Raising Cain, *1992*

582

My mother used to say that there are no strangers, only friends you haven't met yet. She's now in a maximum-security twilight home.

—Dame Edna Everage (Barry Humphries)

583

My parents keep asking why I never come home for a visit. It's because Delta Airlines won't wait in the yard while I run in.

—Margaret Smith

584

My mother was a ventriloquist. For ten years I thought the dog was telling me to kill my father.

—Wendy Liebman

585

I'm probably as good a mother as the next repressed, obsessive-compulsive paranoiac.

—Anne Lamott

586

The sins of the fathers are often visited upon the sons-in-law.

—*John Kiser*

587

Do your kids a favor. Don't have any.

—*Robert Orben*

588

If you just want a wonderful little creature to love, get a puppy.

—*Barbara Walters*

589

Parents are the bones that children sharpen their teeth on.

—*Peter Ustinov (1921–2004)*

590

Alligators have the right idea. They eat their young.

—*Eve Arden (1908–1990)*

591

Never buy anything you can't make your children carry.

—Bill Bryson

592

I asked my mother if I was adopted and she said, "Not yet, but we've placed an ad."

—Dana Snow

593

When I was a child, I got lost in a mall and was raised by saleswomen.

—Rita Rudner

594

Children will quote you correctly only if it is something you wish you hadn't said.

—*Jesse Andrews*

595

Even when freshly washed and relieved of all obvious confections, children tend to be sticky.

—*Fran Lebowitz*

596

As the youngest in the family, I was always getting beat up by the oldest: my mom and dad.

—*Tom Cotter*

597

On my sixteenth birthday, my parents tried to surprise me with a car, but they missed.

—*Tom Cotter*

598

When playing cowboys and Indians, I always wanted to be an Indian so I could have my own casino.

—*Brian Kiley*

599

Adolescence is just one big walking pimple.

—*Carol Burnett*

600

Adolescence is located in the foothills of Jackass Mountain.

—*William Fuerste (1923–2011)*

601

I like children if they're properly cooked.

—*W. C. Fields (1880–1946)*

602

I had too many children. The playpen looked like a bus stop for midgets and was so damp a rainbow formed above it.

—*Phyllis Diller*

603

If you are willing to have children, rhythm is probably the best method of contraception.

—*Elizabeth Hawes*

604

Oh, what a tangled web we weave
When we think our children are naïve.

—Ogden Nash (1902–1971)

605

Advice from children:

Never try to dress your cat.
Never eat a magnet when you have braces.
Never go swimming at Reptile Land.
Never live in a house with one bathroom and three sisters.

—Gathered by schoolteacher Robert Bender

606

Until I was thirteen, I thought my name was Shuddup.

—Daniel Tosh

607

My folks were really strict. When I was bad, they made me sit on a chair facing the coroner.

—George Hrab

608

Only the young die good.

—Oliver Herford (1863–1935)

609

Humpty Dumpty had a great fall. I blame the parents. If your family name was Dumpty, would you name your child Humpty?

—Gary Gulman

610

Why did they send all the king's horses to help put Humpty Dumpty back together again? You need thumbs for that kind of work.

—Gary Gulman

MOTHERS

611

My mother never saw the irony in calling me a son of a bitch.

—*Richard Jeni (1957–2007)*

612

When I was born, my mother told me they threw away the mold. But it grew back.

—*Emo Philips*

613

Mother, food, love, and career are the four major guilt groups.

—*Cathy Guisewite*

614

I'd probably be overly protective as a mother. I wouldn't let the kid out of my body.

—*Wendy Liebman*

615

When I was a baby, my father would throw me up in the air and then answer the phone.

—Rita Rudner

616

My parents sent my baby picture to *Ripley's Believe It or Not*. They sent it back with a note saying they didn't believe it.

—Joan Rivers

617

Don't take your baby to bed with you because you might roll over on it and strain your back.

—Harry Hill

618

My mother was an authority on pigsties. She would look at my room and say, "This is the worst pigsty I've ever seen."

—Bill Cosby

619

You've buttered your bread, now sleep in it.

—*Gracie Allen (1895–1964)*

620

Mothers are a biological necessity. Fathers are a social invention.

—*Margaret Mead (1901–1978)*

621

I bought my mother-in-law a chair, but she wouldn't let me plug it in.

—*Henny Youngman (1906–1998)*

622

If evolution really works, how come mothers have only two hands?

—*Ed Dussault*

623

A sweater is a garment worn by a child when the mother feels cold.

—*Cuzzie Ottavi (1920–2005)*

624

Any mother could do the jobs of several air-traffic controllers with ease.

—Lisa Alther

625

My mother-in-law has had so many face-lifts that she has a slipknot on top of her head.

—Claudia Sherman

626

In order to influence a child, be careful not to be that child's parent.

—Don Marquis (1878–1937)

627

A hen is an egg's way of making another egg.

—Samuel Butler (1835–1902)

628

We want our children to fit in and to stand out, even though the goals are conflicting.

—Ellen Goodman

629

My mother said that honesty is the best policy and that money isn't everything. She was wrong about other things, too.

—Gerald Barzan

630

At the mall I saw a kid on a leash. If I ever have a kid, it's gonna be cordless.

—Wendy Liebman

631

Should a woman give birth after thirty-five? Thirty-five is enough kids for anybody.

—Gracie Allen (1895–1964)

DIVORCE

632

In the old days, divorce was rare. People got married and stuck it out until it killed them.

—*Leo Roberts*

633

I never heard of a trial separation that didn't work.

—*Lawrence Block*

634

We tried macrobiotics, we tried crystals, we tried meditation. Finally we tried divorce. That worked.

—*Cartoonist Bruce Eric Kaplan*

635

People often ask how short I am. After my last divorce, I was about $100,000 short.

—Mickey Rooney

636

Half of all marriages end in divorce. And then there are the really unhappy ones.

—Joan Rivers

637

Just another one of our many disagreements. He wants a no-fault divorce, whereas I would prefer to have the bastard crucified.

—Cartoon caption by
J. B. Handelsman (1922–2007)

638

Divorce . . . from a Latin word meaning to rip out a man's genitals through his wallet.

—Robin Williams

639

Divorces are expensive, but they're worth it.

—Willie Nelson

640

Without love there wouldn't be so many divorces.

—Edgar Watson Howe (1853–1937)

641

My marriage didn't work out. I was a human being and he was a Klingon.

—Carol Leifer

642

I'm at an age when I just want to settle down and have my first divorce.

—Peter J. Fogel

643

I don't believe in divorce. I believe in widowhood.

—Carolyn Green

644

Remarrying a husband you've divorced is like having your appendix put back in.

—*Phyllis Diller*

645

I was raised by my mother because my dad died when I was eight years old. At least that's what he told us in the letter.

—*Drew Carey*

646

When I was thirty years old, my mother was still trying to have an abortion.

—*Jim Bailey imitating Phyllis Diller*

647

My divorce was messy because there was a child involved. My husband.

—*Wendy Liebman*

648

When a woman gets a divorce, I believe she should give back the ring and keep the stone.

—*Zsa Zsa Gabor*

649

Love is grand. Divorce is a hundred grand.

—*Unknown*

650

My husband and I divorced over religious differences. He thought he was God and I didn't.

—*Maxine, the Crabby Lady (John Wagner)*

651

The only time my wife and I had simultaneous orgasms was when the judge signed the divorce papers.

—*Woody Allen*

652

My wife doesn't understand me. She only speaks Swahili.

—*Tim Conway*

653

I've never been married, but I tell people I'm divorced so they won't think something's wrong with me.

—Elayne Boosler

654

I know what women want. Her lawyer told me.

—Cartoon caption by Leo Cullum (1942–2010)

655

I'm friends with all my exes, apart from husbands.

—Cher

656

Alimony is like buying oats for a dead horse.

—Arthur "Bugs" Baer (1886–1969)

RELIGION

657

I'm worried that the universe will soon need replacing. It's not holding a charge.

—*Edward Chilton*

658

The universe is a big place, perhaps the biggest.

—*Kurt Vonnegut (1922–2007)*

659

In the beginning, the universe was created. This has been widely regarded as a bad move.

—*Douglas Adams (1952–2001)*

660

The universe never did make sense. I suspect it was built on government contract.

—*Robert Heinlein (1907–1988)*

661

Pity the meek, for they shall inherit the earth.

—Don Marquis (1878–1937)

662

Maybe this world is another planet's hell.

—Aldous Huxley (1894–1963)

663

The world is in a mess because God sent his only begotten son. He should have come himself.

—From The Dam *(1981), a novel by Robert Byrne*

664

God sometimes gives nuts to toothless people.

—Matt Groening

665

Why does evil exist? To thicken the plot.

—Indian saint Ramakrishna (1836–1886)

666

They say that God is everywhere, and yet we always think of him as somewhat of a recluse.

—Emily Dickinson (1830–1886)

667

I read the book of Job last night. I don't think God comes off very well.

—Virginia Woolf (1882–1941)

668

In the beginning there was nothing and God said, "Let there be light." There was still nothing, but you could see it better.

—Ellen DeGeneres

669

In the garden of Eden, Eve said to Adam, "Does this leaf make me look fat?"

—Red Buttons (1919–2006)

670

The first time Adam had a chance, he laid the blame on a woman.

—*Lady Nancy Astor (1879–1964)*

671

If there were a Divine Power, all the world's oil would be under Denmark.

—*A friend of Calvin Trillin's*

672

I may not believe in God, but I don't ring doorbells to say I'm a Seventh-Day Atheist.

—*Dr. Thomas Eisner (1929–2011)*

673

I don't know if God exists, but it would be better for his reputation if he didn't.

—*Jules Renard (1864–1910)*

674

I'm halfway through Genesis and quite appalled by the disgraceful behavior of all the characters, including God.

—*J. R. Ackerley (1896–1967)*

675

If God exists, I hope he has a good excuse.

—Woody Allen

676

Atheism is a nonprophet organization.

—George Carlin (1937–2008)

677

O God, if there is a God, have mercy on my soul, if there is a soul.

—Frederick II (1712–1786)

678

I am ashamed to confess that I have nothing to confess.

—Fanny Burney (1752–1840)

679

There can be no Creator because his grief at the fate of his creation would be inconceivable and unendurable.

—Elias Canetti (1905–1994)

680

Our only hope is the off chance that God exists.

—Alice Thomas Ellis (1932–2005)

681

Some say there is a God, others say there is no God. The truth probably lies somewhere in between.

—William Butler Yeats (1865–1939)

682

I talked to the Holy Spirit last night and he didn't look at all well. He was pale as a ghost.

—Leo Roberts

683

Religion backed up by commerce is awful hard for a heathen to overcome.

—Will Rogers (1879–1935)

684

If there is a God, why is the church organist so lousy?

—Pianist Earl Wild at age ten (1915–2010)

685

You can't imagine the extra work I had when I was God.

—Hirohito (1901–1989), once emperor of Japan

686

What if God turns out to be a giant chicken? What then?

—Cartoonist Bill Watterson

687

God always has another custard pie up his sleeve.

—Lynn Redgrave (1943–2010)

688

If your prayers were always answered, you'd have reason to doubt the wisdom of God.

—*Unknown*

689

Being omniscient, God knew Murphy's Law. On the eighth day of creation, God said, "Okay, Murphy, take over."

—*Robert Silvestri*

690

The meaning of eternity can't be fully understood until you've heard expert witnesses testify.

—*Stan Silbeg*

691

The world can't end today because it's already tomorrow in Australia.

—*Charles Schulz (1922–2000)*

692

If God doesn't destroy Hollywood Boulevard, he owes Sodom and Gomorrah an apology.

—*Jay Leno*

693

If God was a Catholic, how come he only had one son?

—*Unknown*

694

I was raised Catholic and received the body and blood of Christ every Sunday at Communion until the age of thirty, when I became a vegetarian.

—*Joe Queenan*

695

The probable fact is that we are descended not only from monkeys but from monks.

—*Elbert Hubbard (1856–1915)*

696

Hearing nuns' confessions is like being stoned to death with popcorn.

—*Bishop Fulton J. Sheen (1895–1979)*

697

I'd rather be a Mormon than a member of a religion that is harder to disprove.

—*Emo Philips*

698

The pope is a disgrace to the dress he wears.

—*Gloria Steinem*

699

The pope's car doesn't have little statues of saints on the dashboard. Just a mirror.

—*Jay Leno*

700

I'm dating the pope. Actually, I'm just dating him to get to God.

—*Judy Tenuta*

701

To all things clergic
I am allergic.

—*Alexander Woollcott (1887–1943)*

702

Bart Simpson says Grace: "Dear God, we paid for all this stuff ourselves, so thanks for nothing."

—*Matt Groening*

703

The atheists have produced a Christmas play. It's called *Coincidence on Thirty-Fourth Street.*

—*Jay Leno*

704

Organized religion is a bureaucracy between man and God.

—*Bill Maher*

705

When Lot's wife looked back at Sodom and was turned into a pillar of salt, she said, "Salt I have, popcorn I need."

—*Red Buttons (1919–2006)*

706

Atheism is not a religion in the same sense that not skiing is a sport.

—*Ricky Gervais*

707

Jesus loves you, but everybody else thinks you're a jerk.

—*Unknown*

708

You think of me as an atheist, but to God I'm the loyal opposition.

—Woody Allen

709

I'm so timid I was beaten up by Quakers.

—Woody Allen

710

When I was a kid I used to pray for a bicycle. Then I realized that the Lord doesn't work that way, so I stole one and asked him to forgive me.

—Emo Philips

711

God is a great humorist, but he has a slow audience.

—Garrison Keillor

712

My goddaughter calls me God for short. That's cute. I taught her that.

—Ellen DeGeneres

713

Lord, give me patience . . . and hurry!

—*George Robinson Ragsdale*

714

Two great European narcotics are alcohol and Christianity.

—*Frederich Nietzsche (1844–1900)*

715

Conscience is a mother-in-law whose visit never ends.

—*H. L. Mencken (1880–1956)*

716

Forgive, O Lord, my little jokes on Thee;
And I'll forgive you for Thy great big one on me.

—*Robert Frost (1874–1963)*

717

The Blessed Virgin Mary, like all Jewish mothers, thought her son was God.

—*Garrison Keillor*

718

An earthquake is God grabbing the world and saying, "Cough!"

—*Unknown*

719

God is love, but get it in writing.

—*Gypsy Rose Lee (1914–1970)*

720

I know I'm God because when I pray to him, I find I'm talking to myself.

—*Peter Barnes (1931–2004)*

721

I don't pray because I don't want God to know where I am.

—*Marsha Doble*

722

Christianity Celebrates One Billionth Unanswered Prayer!

—*Headline in the* Onion

723

For better results, pray to the devil.

—*Jim Loy*

724

God could end misery in the world, but if he did, nobody would speak to him.

—*Bill Maher*

725

The Old Testament God should have signed up for an anger-management class.

—*Lewis Black*

726

Dear God, with your help I'm starving to death.

—*From* Fiddler on the Roof

727

Now there's a politically correct Bible. Jesus is killed by secondhand smoke.

—*Adam Ferrara*

728

Unless you sin, Jesus died for nothing.

—*Unknown*

729

I spent the first twenty years of my life waiting for two men I was reasonably certain would never come back: my daddy and Jesus. At least with Jesus I knew he wasn't gone because of something I did.

—*Brett Butler*

730

I'm the second-most famous person from Timmins, Ontario, after Shania Twain. That's like being the second-most famous person from Nazareth. Who cares about Duncan of Nazareth?

—*Derek Edwards*

731

I went to a convent in New York and was expelled for my insistence that the Immaculate Conception was spontaneous combustion.

—*Dorothy Parker (1893–1967)*

732

My wife and I agree about God. We respect His privacy and go about our business.

—*Steve Rubenstein*

733

You can safely assume that you've created God in your own image when it turns out that God hates all the same people you do.

—*Anne Lamott*

734

One of the worst things is having to kill a family member because they are the devil. But otherwise it's been a pretty good day.

—Emo Philips

735

His teeth were like the Ten Commandments: all broken.

—Herbert Beerbohm Tree (1852–1917)

736

Moses was a basket case.

—Unknown

737

Saints need sinners.

—Alan Watts (1915–1973)

738

Most saints live to regret their career choice.

—Bob Stokes

739

It's hard to be religious when certain people are not struck by lightning.

—Calvin and Hobbes *(Bill Watterson)*

740

In grade school, a nun told me to get closer to Jesus, so I became a Jew.

—*Sunda Croonquist*

741

Religious wars are to see who has the better imaginary friend.

—*John Wing*

742

I have the greatest respect towards everybody's religious obligations, never mind how comical.

—*Herman Melville (1819–1891)*

743

Religion gives people hope in a world torn apart by religion.

—*Jon Stewart*

744

Blasphemy is a victimless crime.

—*Salman Rushdie*

745

The early Christians got the best lions.

—*Unknown*

746

Fundamentalists are to Christianity as paint-by-numbers is to art.

—Robin Tyler

747

It was wonderful being born again, but I don't think my mother enjoyed it much.

—John Wing

748

I'm a paranoid agnostic. I don't think God exists, but I'm sure there is some sort of force out there working against me.

—Marc Maron

749

I'm not normally a praying man, but if you're up there, please save me, Superman!

—From The Simpsons *(Matt Groening)*

750

Going to church no more makes you a Christian than standing in a garage makes you a car.

—*Variously ascribed*

751

At a religious convention you rub elbows with people you wouldn't rub anywhere else.

—*Unknown*

752

If you don't believe in life after death, you've never been to the suburbs.

—*Cecil Adams*

753

Heaven is a gated community.

—*Peter Steiner*

754

Heaven sounds boring. Maybe they let you go to hell on weekends.

—*Javier Bardem*

755

The average man, who does not know what to do with this life, wants another one that will last forever.

—*Anatole France (1844–1924)*

756

Everybody wants to go to heaven, but nobody wants to die.

—*Unknown*

757

I don't suppose there is any chance of rain?

—*Joan of Arc (1412–1431)*

758

The only thing worse than religion is getting hit by lightning for criticizing it.

—*Jim Loy*

759

A halo has to fall just a few inches to become a noose.

—*Father Guido Sarducci (Larry Lorenzoni)*

760

If a man wants to make a million dollars, the best way would be to start his own religion.

—L. Ron Hubbard (1911–1986) in 1946, before he founded Scientology

761

An open mind is a virtue, but not so open that your brains fall out.

—James Oberg

762

Monday is the root of all evil.

—Jim Loy

763

Good people sleep better than bad people, but bad people enjoy being awake more.

—Woody Allen

764

Dial-a-Prayer hung up on me.

—Jackie Vernon (1924–1987)

765

Frisbeetarianism is the belief that when you die your soul gets stuck on the roof.

—*George Carlin (1937–2008)*

766

When I think of all the harm the Bible has done, I despair of ever writing anything to equal it.

—*Oscar Wilde (1854–1900)*

767

The devil is an optimist if he thinks he can make people worse than they are.

—*Karl Kraus (1874–1936)*

768

Blameless people are always the most exasperating.

—*George Eliot (Mary Anne Evans, 1819–1880)*

769

I attend an atheist church. People testify that they used to be crippled and still are.

—*Paula Poundstone*

770

A celibate clergy is a good idea because it tends to suppress any hereditary propensity toward fanaticism.

—Carl Sagan (1934–1996)

771

Life in Lubbock, Texas, taught me two things. One is that God loves you and you're going to burn in hell. The other is that sex is the most awful, filthy thing there is and you should save it for someone you love.

—Butch Hancock

772

SAVE YOU? GOD CAN'T EVEN CURE ACNE.

—Favorite bumper sticker of atheist Madalyn Murray O'Hare (1919–1995)

773

If God is your copilot, swap seats.

—Unknown

774

I don't compare myself to Jesus, but there are spooky similarities.

—*Dame Edna Everage (Barry Humphries)*

775

For Lent I gave up hope.

—*Danny Bevins*

776

For Lent I gave up Catholicism.

—*Stephen Colbert*

777

One angel in heaven to another: "I applied for reincarnation, but unless you know computers, you can forget about it."

—*Robert Mankoff*

778

I went to a church in Chicago that had six commandments and four do-the-best-you-cans.

—*Comedian George Wallace*

779

If somebody predicts that the world is about to end, my advice is to keep on flossing.

—Michael Smerconish

780

A radical Islamic cleric said earthquakes are caused by women in revealing clothing. Scientists said that it's worth it.

—Jimmy Fallon

781

And the Lord spoke to the children of Israel and said, "Thou must forswear these practices, which are an abomination, you know what I'm saying?"

—Cartoon caption by Lee Lorenz

782

Jews can't serve on juries because they insist they're guilty.

—Cathy Ladman

783

Moses dragged us through the desert to the one place in the Middle East where there is no oil.

—Golda Meir (1898–1978)

784

Jews don't go camping. Life is hard enough already.

—Carol Siskind

785

Oy to the world.

—Jewish Christmas carol

786

Yo.

—Lament from a dyslexic Jew

787

Jews don't drink much because it interferes with their suffering.

—Milton Berle (1908–2002)

788

To my grandfather, gentiles were people who sold their children for whiskey.

—*David Steinberg*

789

My grandfather was a juggler in a Russian circus. He was able to worry about six things at once.

—*Richard Lewis*

790

Jews are born with guilt. Catholics learn it in school.

—*Elayne Boosler*

791

Unlike Christians, Jews don't use bumper stickers. You never see HONK IF YOU LOVE MOSES.

—*Gregg Rogell*

792

Judaism is Christianity's cranky grandpa.

—*Stephen Colbert*

793

My husband was never circumcised because the doctors were afraid of brain damage.

—*Claudia Krevek*

794

My people wandered in the wilderness for forty years because even in biblical times men would not stop to ask for directions.

—*Elayne Boosler*

795

Whenever a person goes into a delicatessen and orders a pastrami on white bread, somewhere a Jew dies.

—*Milton Berle (1908–2002)*

796

Jews killed Christ, but it was only for three days.

—*Lenny Bruce (1925–1966)*

797

When God commanded Abraham to circumcise himself, Abraham said, "Why not? It's no skin off my nose."

—*Red Buttons (1919–2006)*

798

The Jews and Arabs should settle their disputes in the true spirit of Christian charity.

—*Alexander Wiley*

799

My mother has a Jewish satellite dish. It picks up problems from other families.

—*Richard Lewis*

800

My mother could make anybody feel guilty. She used to get letters of apology from people she didn't even know.

—*Joan Rivers*

LIFE

801

Imagination and fiction make up more than three-quarters of our real life.

—*Simone Weil (1909–1943)*

802

Life is a short visit to a toy shop between birth and death.

—*Desmond Morris*

803

It's never too late, in fiction or in life, to revise.

—*Nancy Thayer*

804

Life is full of misery, loneliness, and suffering—and it's all over much too soon.

—*Woody Allen*

805

I get mail, therefore I am.

—Dilbert *(Scott Adams)*

806

Life is one long process of getting tired.

—Samuel Butler (1835–1902)

807

If at first you do succeed, try something harder.

—*Ann Landers (1918–2002)*

808

Life is better than death because it's less boring and there are fresh peaches.

—*Alice Walker*

809

Time is a dressmaker specializing in alterations.

—*Faith Baldwin (1893–1978)*

810

Men love women, women love children, children love hamsters. It's quite hopeless.

—*Alice Thomas Ellis (1932–2005)*

811

It's weak and despicable to want things and not try to get them.

—*Joanna Field (1900–1998)*

812

The secret of life is to just hang around until you get used to it.

—Charlie Brown (Charles Schulz, 1922–2000)

813

If life gives you lemons, squirt the juice in people's eyes.

—Leo Roberts

814

Life is a sexually transmitted terminal disease.

—Unknown

815

Life is too short for traffic.

—Dan Bellack

816

Learn to drink the cup of life without stirring up the bottom.

—Carlotta Monterey O'Neill (1888–1970)

817

Life is a game played on us while we are playing other games.

—*Evan Esar (1899–1995)*

818

Life is a shipwreck, but we must not forget to sing in the lifeboats.

—*Voltaire (1694–1778)*

819

Life is uncertain. Eat dessert first.

—*Ernestine Ulmer*

820

You are excess baggage in the airport of life.

—*Judy Tenuta*

821

This life is a test; it is only a test. If it were a real life, you would receive instructions on where to go and what to do.

—*Unknown*

822

In the book of life, the answers aren't in the back.

—Charlie Brown (Charles Schulz, 1922–2000)

823

The purpose of life is to fight maturity.

—Dick Werthimer (1929–1999)

824

Life is a moderately good play with a badly written third act.

—Truman Capote (1924–1984)

825

If you reduce your expectations to zero, life becomes a series of happy surprises.

—Tuck Andres

826

Not only is life a bitch, it has puppies.

—Adrienne Gusoff

827

Sometimes I lie awake at night and ask, "Where have I gone wrong?" Then a voice says, "This is going to take more than one night."

—*Charlie Brown (Charles Schulz, 1922–2000)*

828

The secret of life is to replace one worry with another.

—*Charlie Brown (Charles Schulz, 1922–2000)*

829

A clean house is a sign of a misspent life.

—*Unknown*

830

If you regret that life is short, don't kill time.

—*Edgar Watson Howe (1853–1937)*

831

It may be that the sole purpose in life is to serve as a warning to others.

—*Steven Wright*

832

Every day is a new beginning and a chance to blow it.

—*Cathy Guisewite*

833

Any idiot can face a crisis—it's the day-to-day living that wears you out.

—*Anton Chekhov (1860–1904)*

834

Living is like licking honey off a thorn.

—*Lisa Wertmuller*

835

Imagination and fiction make up three-quarters of life.

—*Simone Weil (1909–1943)*

836

Humanity is a virus in shoes.

—*Bill Hicks (1961–1994)*

837

Nothing is more precious than teeming, overabundant, resource-destroying human life.

—*From the* Onion

838

People change and forget to tell each other.

—*Lillian Hellman (1905–1984)*

839

The most exhausting thing in life is being insincere. That's why so much social life is exhausting.

—*Anne Morrow Lindbergh (1906–2001)*

840

A flaw in the human character is that everybody wants to build and nobody wants to do maintenance.

—*Kurt Vonnegut (1922–2007)*

841

You can't build a reputation on what you intend to do.

—*Liz Smith*

842

If all the world's a stage, I want to operate the trapdoor.

—*Paul Beatty*

843

All the world's a cage.

—*Jeanne Phillips*

844

Life is like a roll of toilet paper. The closer to the end you get, the faster it goes.

—*Andy Rooney (1919–2011)*

845

How is it possible to find meaning in a finite world given my waist and shirt size?

—*Woody Allen*

846

Humankind can't stand too much reality.

—*T. S. Eliot (1888–1965)*

847

Reality is what doesn't go away when you stop believing in it.

—*Philip K. Dick (1928–1982)*

848

Reality is something you rise above.

—*Liza Minnelli*

849

Reality is the leading cause of stress for those in touch with it.

—*Jane Wagner*

850

I can handle reality in small doses, but as a lifestyle it's much too confining.

—*Lily Tomlin*

851

Idealism is fine, but as it approaches reality, the cost becomes prohibitive.

—*William F. Buckley, Jr. (1925–2008)*

852

A deep understanding of reality is the same thing as laziness. You never see a statue of Buddha jogging.

—*Scott Adams*

853

Reality is a temporary illusion brought on by an absence of beer.

—*Unknown*

854

Reality continues to ruin my life.

—Calvin and Hobbes *(Bill Watterson)*

855

The difference between reality and fiction is that fiction has to make sense.

—*Unknown*

856

In the 1960s, people took acid to make the world seem weird. Now that the world is weird, people take Prozac to make it seem normal.

—*Unknown*

857

I believe in looking reality straight in the eye and denying it.

—*Garrison Keillor*

858

Reality has a well-known liberal bias.

—*Stephen Colbert*

CONVERSATION

859

Conversation is when three people are talking. Gossip is when one of them leaves.

—*Andy Dappen*

860

Most conversations are simply monologues delivered in the presence of a witness.

—*Margaret Millar (1915–1994)*

861

The first thing I do in the morning is brush my teeth and sharpen my tongue.

—*Oscar Levant (1906–1972)*

862

We will talk without listening to each other, which is the best way to get along.

—*Alfred de Musset (1810–1857)*

863

There is no such thing as conversation. There are intersecting monologues.

—*Rebecca West (1892–1983)*

864

A good listener is a good talker with a sore throat.

—*Katharine Whitehorn*

865

A good listener is not only popular everywhere, but after a while knows something.

—*Wilson Mizner (1876–1933)*

866

Of those who say nothing, few are silent.

—*Thomas Neill (1826–1885)*

867

Years ago there were things you could not say in front of a girl. Today you can say them but you can't say "girl."

—*Tom Lehrer*

868

A good listener is usually thinking about something else.

—*Kin Hubbard (1868–1930)*

869

Nobody ever listened to reason on an empty stomach.

—*Kin Hubbard (1868–1930)*

870

The term *lady* is most often used to describe someone you wouldn't want to talk to for even five minutes.

—*Fran Lebowitz*

871

Charm is a way of getting the answer yes without having asked any clear question.

—*Albert Camus (1913–1960)*

872

People rarely get into trouble by listening too much.

—Dr. Mardy Grothe

873

We would rather criticize ourselves than not talk about ourselves at all.

—François La Rochefoucauld (1613–1680)

874

If you want to get your message across, shut up.

—Dr. Mardy Grothe

875

You never see a fish on a wall with its mouth shut.

—Sally Berger

876

By whom?

—Dorothy Parker (1893–1967),
when told she was outspoken

877

It is a common delusion that you can make things better by talking about them.

—*Dame Rose Macaulay (1881–1958)*

878

Talking about your troubles is no good. Eighty percent of your friends don't care and the rest are glad.

—*Tommy Lasorda*

879

How time flies when you do all the talking!

—*Harvey Fierstein,* Torch Song Trilogy, *1979*

880

Arguments are to be avoided. They are always vulgar and often convincing.

—*Oscar Wilde (1854–1900)*

881

No one has a finer command of language than the person who keeps his mouth shut.

—*Sam Rayburn (1882–1961)*

882

Silence is one of the hardest arguments to refute.

—*Josh Billings (1818–1885)*

883

My wife and I had words, but I never got to use mine.

—*Fibber McGee (Bob Sweeney, 1918–1992)*

884

Conversation would be much improved by the frequent use of three words: I don't know.

—*André Maurois (1885–1967)*

885

I won't insult your intelligence by suggesting that you really believe what you just said.

—*William F. Buckley, Jr. (1925–2008)*

886

He has occasional flashes of silence that make his conversation delightful.

—*Sydney Smith (1771–1845)*

887

March is a windy month. Help out by keeping your yap shut from time to time.

—Maxine, the Crabby Lady (John Wagner)

888

The fun of talk is finding out what a man really thinks and then contrasting it with lies he has been telling all his life.

—Benjamin Disraeli (1804–1881)

EDUCATION

889

What are schools for if not for indoctrination against communism?

—*Richard Nixon (1913–1994)*

890

Education is the ability to listen to almost anything without losing your temper.

—*Robert Frost (1874–1963)*

891

A lack of education is an extraordinary handicap when one is being offensive.

—*Josephine Tey (1896–1952)*

892

I speak Esperanto like a native.

—*Spike Milligan (1918–2002)*

893

An intellectual is a person who has discovered something more interesting than sex.

—*Aldous Huxley (1894–1963)*

894

Historians are like deaf people who go on answering questions that nobody has asked.

—*Leo Tolstoy (1828–1910)*

895

When I was in school, there was no Ritalin for attention deficit disorder, just a big nun with a ruler.

—*Maureen Dowd*

896

My school was so rough the school newspaper had an obituary section.

—*Norm Crosby*

897

My act is very educational. The other night a man who was leaving said, "Well, that taught me a lesson."

—*Daniel Tosh*

898

I had an education a nun would envy. Until I was fifteen, I was more familiar with Africa than with my own body.

—*Joe Orton (1933–1967)*

899

"Whom are you?" said he, for he had been to night school.

—*George Ade (1866–1944)*

900

In one generation we went from teaching Latin and Greek to remedial English.

—*Joseph Sobran (1946–2010)*

901

A professor is someone who talks in other people's sleep.

—*W. H. Auden (1907–1973)*

902

Sex education in school may be a good idea, but there should be no homework.

—*Bill Cosby*

903

The No Child Left Behind law is being replaced by one called "Some kids are just duds."

—*Jimmy Fallon*

904

I quit school in the sixth grade because of pneumonia, not because I had it but because I couldn't spell it.

—*Rocky Graziano (1919–1990)*

905

The ideal gift for the high school graduate is a job.

—*Evan Esar (1899–1995)*

906

The difference between a teacher and a pizza is that the pizza can feed a family of four.

—*Mark Russell*

907

The great universities take in ten thousand plums and turn out ten thousand prunes.

—*Frank Lloyd Wright (1867–1959)*

908

There is nothing on earth for innocent people so horrible as a school. In prison, for example, the prisoners aren't forced to read books written by the wardens.

—George Bernard Shaw (1856–1950)

909

American students are like American colleges. Both have half-dead faculties.

—James Thurber (1894–1961)

910

A university is what a college becomes when the faculty loses interest in the students.

—John Ciardi (1916–1986)

911

People are born ignorant, not stupid. They are made stupid by education.

—Bertrand Russell (1872–1970)

912

I majored in nursing but I had to drop out. I ran out of milk.

—Judy Tenuta

913

Americans of the future will need to know Spanish to give instructions and Chinese to take instructions.

—Argus Hamilton

914

You know there's a problem with our education system when you realize that of the three R's only one starts with *R*.

—Dennis Miller

915

Teach me to be an engineer. I don't care if it takes all day.

—Dilbert *(Scott Adams)*

916

In high school, I was a fetus with shoes.

—Dana Carvey

917

My school was so tough we had our own coroner. We wrote essays on what we wanted to be if we grew up.

—Lenny Bruce (1925–1966)

918

I attended a school for emotionally disturbed teachers.

—Woody Allen

919

You shouldn't have to go to high school until you are at least forty, you've had a lot of therapy, and you're ready for it.

—Marilyn Kentz

920

I'm never going to be a movie star, but then Elizabeth Taylor is never going to teach first grade.

—*Mary H. Wilson (1933–2007)*

921

My daughter goes to SMU instead of UCLA because it was one less letter to remember.

—*Shecky Greene*

922

When a subject becomes totally obsolete, we make it a required course.

—*Peter Drucker (1909–2005)*

923

Life is too short to explain the obvious to idiots.

—*Gloria Naylor*

924

What counts is what you learn after you know it all.

—*Earl Weaver*

925

Everybody is ignorant, only on different subjects.

—*Will Rogers (1879–1935)*

926

Eggheads! What do they know?

—*Homer Simpson (Matt Groening)*

927

The average PhD thesis is nothing but the transference of bones from one graveyard to another.

—*J. Frank Dobie (1888–1964)*

928

Time is a great teacher, but it kills all of its students.

—*Hector Berlioz (1803–1869)*

929

In my school you were searched for guns and knives on the way in, and if you didn't have any, you were given some.

—*Emo Philips*

930

I was an honor student. "Yes, Your Honor. No, Your Honor."

—*Red Buttons (1919–2006)*

931

I got an A in philosophy because I proved that my professor didn't exist.

—*Judy Tenuta*

932

Benjamin Franklin said the fish and guests smell after three days. Old friends from college smell already.

—*P. J. O'Rourke*

933

I was a fantastic student until age ten, when my mind began to wander.

—*Grace Paley (1922–2007)*

934

Education begins by teaching children to read and ends up by making most of them hate reading.

—*Holbrook Jackson (1874–1948)*

935

As long as there is algebra, there will be prayer in school.

—*Larry Miller*

936

English was good enough for Jesus Christ and it's good enough for the children of Texas.

—*Texas Governor Miriam "Ma" Ferguson (1875–1961) in 1924*

HAPPINESS

937

Make somebody happy today: mind your own business.

—*Ann Landers (1918–2002)*

938

There is nothing more tedious than a constant round of gaiety.

—*Margery Sharp (1905–1991)*

939

Happy people don't have to have fun.

—*Jean Stafford (1915–1979)*

940

The mouth of a perfectly happy man is filled with beer.

—*Egyptian proverb*

941

My motto is the same as my blood type. B positive.

—*Cynthia Nelms*

942

In times of joy, we all wish we had a tail we could wag.

—*W. H. Auden (1907–1973)*

943

If only we'd stop trying to be happy, we could have a pretty good time.

—*Edith Wharton (1862–1937)*

944

Whenever something good happens to me, I wait two weeks before telling anybody because I like to use the word *fortnight.*

—*Demetri Martin*

945

Happiness is an agreeable sensation arising from contemplating the misery of others.

—*Ambrose Bierce (1842–1914)*

946

My girlfriend bought me a down jacket because it fit my personality.

—Jay London

947

It was such a beautiful day I forgot to be unhappy.

—Frances Noyes Hart (1890–1943)

948

One-half of the world cannot understand the pleasures of the other half.

—Jane Austen (1775–1817)

949

The way to be happy is to live well beyond your means.

—Ruth Gordon (1896–1985)

950

If ignorance is bliss, why aren't there more happy people?

—Philip Howard

951

I'm a paranoid in reverse. I suspect people of plotting to make me happy.

—*J. D. Salinger (1919–2010)*

952

Nobody cares if you're miserable, so you might as well be happy.

—*Cynthia Nelms*

953

The best things in life are silly.

—Dilbert *(Scott Adams)*

954

It's never too late to have a happy childhood.

—*Berke Breathed (*Opus*)*

955

I can think of nothing less pleasurable than a life devoted to pleasure.

—*John D. Rockefeller (1839–1937)*

956

Who says blondes have more fun? I have fun no matter what color my hair is.

—Ruth Parrish

957

It's hard to tell what brings happiness. Poverty and wealth have both failed.

—Frank McKinney Hubbard (1868–1930)

958

Sometimes when I'm depressed, I get a pregnancy test so I can say, "Well, at least I'm not pregnant."

—Daniel Tosh

BEAUTY

959

Being born beautiful is like being born rich and getting steadily poorer.

—*Joan Collins*

960

It's always darkest before the dawn, and then the wrinkles show up.

—*Cathy Guisewite*

961

A woman's best beauty aid is a nearsighted man.

—*Yoko Ono*

962

Last night I laughed the complexion off my face.

—*Elizabeth Longford (1906–2002)*

963

Human beings are 68 percent water, and with some the rest is collagen.

—*Martin Mull*

964

Plastic surgery won't help, but plastic explosives might.

—*Unknown*

965

Beauty is only a light switch away.

—*Unknown*

966

Beauty is in the eye of the cuckolder.

—*Robert Byrne*

967

Just because I'm homely doesn't mean I'm dumb. It's just a coincidence.

—*Unknown*

968

I loaned a friend $8,000 for cosmetic surgery and now I don't know what he looks like.

—*Emo Philips*

969

It's difficult to reconcile the concept that truth is beauty with orthodontia and nose jobs.

—*Judith Viorst*

970

I have to look beautiful so that the poor Filipinos will have a star to look at from their slums.

—*Imelda Marcos*

971

Ladies! Never let your mother comb your hair when she's mad at your dad.

—*Gallagher*

972

Ever have one of those nights when you didn't want to go out but your hair looked too good to stay home?

—*Jack Simmons*

973

Beauty, like male ballet dancers, makes some men afraid.

—Mordecai Richler (1931–2001)

974

After forty, a woman has to choose between her face and her figure. My advice is to choose your face and stay sitting down.

—Barbara Cartland (1901–2000)

975

How can women pour hot wax on their legs, then pull their hair out by the roots, and still be afraid of a spider?

—*Jerry Seinfeld*

976

My girlfriend got a bad haircut and cried for two hours. I said, "What are you crying about? It's only a haircut. I'm the one who has to get a new girlfriend."

—*Anthony Jeselnik*

977

I'm not bald, I'm a person of scalp.

—*Unknown*

978

I'm not really bald. I'm a hair donor.

—*Clifford Kuhn*

979

The most delightful advantage of being bald is that you can hear snowflakes.

—*R. G. Daniels*

980

Bald women have more time.

—*Chet Hurley*

981

Hair is the bane of most women's lives.

—*Joan Collins*

982

If you're bald, remember that grass doesn't grow on a busy street.

—*William Hague*

983

There is no such thing as a good comb-over.

—*Charles Low*

984

I bought a book on hair loss and the pages kept falling out.

—*Jay London*

985

I knew I was going bald because it was taking longer and longer to wash my face.

—*Harry Hill*

986

It is foolish to tear out one's hair in grief, as though sorrow is less with baldness.

—*Cicero (106–43 BC)*

FOOD

987

If you don't show up at a party, people will assume you're fat.

—*From* Newhart

988

You know you're getting fat if your car doesn't fit.

—*Cynthia Nelms*

989

A real friend won't go on a diet if you are fat.

—*Erma Bombeck (1927–1996)*

990

Diets are for people who are thick and tired of it.

—*Mary Tyler Moore*

991

In general, my children refused to eat anything that hadn't danced on TV.

—Erma Bombeck (1927–1996)

992

Where's my purse? I think I still have a fatburger in there.

—Bette Midler

993

If you can't tell a spoon from a ladle, you're fat.

—*Demetri Martin*

994

I'm on a Valium diet. I take four at breakfast, and for the rest of the day food keeps falling out of my mouth.

—*Max Alexander*

995

I was on a diet for fourteen days. I lost exactly two weeks.

—*Sam Levenson (1911–1980)*

996

At mealtime, my mother gave the family a choice: take it or leave it.

—*Robert Orben*

997

A luncheon is a lunch that lasts an eon.

—*Miss Manners (Judith Martin)*

998

Cooking is like love. It should be entered into with abandon or not at all.

—Harriet Van Horn (1920–1998)

999

What my mother believed about cooking is that if you worked hard and prospered, someone else would do it for you.

—Nora Ephron

1,000

I don't watch cooking shows on television. At the end they hold the food up to the camera and say, "Here it is. It's delicious. You can't have any. Thanks for watching. Good-bye."

—Jerry Seinfeld

1,001

The Bible says don't eat pork. Is that God speaking or just pigs trying to outsmart everybody?

—Jon Stewart

1,002

In supermarkets, Soup for One is always eight aisles away from Party Mix.

—*Elayne Boosler*

1,003

My theory is that all Scottish food is based on a dare.

—*Mike Myers*

1,004

If you can't control your peanut butter, you can't control your life.

—*Bill Watterson*

1,005

My husband thinks that health food is anything he eats before the expiration date.

—*Rita Rudner*

1,006

Bread that must be cut with an ax is bread that is too nourishing.

—*Fran Lebowitz*

1,007

Health food makes me sick.

—*Calvin Trillin*

1,008

I went to a restaurant that served "breakfast at any time." I ordered French toast during the Renaissance.

—*Steven Wright*

1,009

Whenever I eat at a German-Chinese restaurant, an hour later I'm hungry for power.

—*Dick Cavett*

1,010

I went out with some people last night for Mexican food, which is really unusual for me because I hate people.

—*Amy Foster*

1,011

Mayonnaise is a sauce that serves the French in place of a state religion.

—*Ambrose Bierce (1842–1914)*

1,012

Never eat anything that has to be explained.

—*Snoopy (Charles Schulz, 1922–2000)*

1,013

What you eat standing up doesn't count.

—*Beth Barnes*

1,014

Food is an important part of a balanced diet.

—*Fran Lebowitz*

1,015

I had to go on two diets at once because one wasn't giving me enough food.

—*Barry Marter*

1,016

I was a vegetarian until I started leaning toward the sun.

—*Rita Rudner*

1,017

I'm not a vegetarian because I love animals. I'm a vegetarian because I hate plants.

—*A. Whitney Brown*

1,018

I am a vegetarian not for my health, but for the health of the chickens.

—*Isaac Bashevis Singer (1904–1991)*

1,019

Vegetarian is an old Indian word meaning "lousy hunter."

—*Andy Rooney (1919–2011)*

1,020

If slaughterhouses had glass walls, everyone would be a vegetarian.

—*Paul McCartney*

1,021

If you water it and it dies, it's a plant. If you pull it out and it grows back, it's a weed.

—*Gallagher*

1,022

Red meat is not bad for you. What's bad is blue-green meat.

—*Tommy Smothers*

1,023

I can't get started in the morning until I've had a cup of hot coffee. Oh, I've tried other enemas.

—*Emo Philips*

1,024

It doesn't take nearly as much water to make good coffee as most people think.

—*Tom Bernard*

1,025

Facts must be faced. Vegetables don't taste as good as most other things do.

—*Peg Bracken (1918–2007)*

1,026

You don't get over hating to cook any more than you get over having big feet.

—*Peg Bracken (1918–2007)*

1,027

I hate skinny women who say things like "Sometimes I forget to eat." You've got to be a special kind of stupid to forget to eat.

—*Marsha Warfield*

1,028

I came from a family where gravy was considered a beverage.

—*Erma Bombeck (1927–1996)*

1,029

A good hostess is like a duck, serene on the surface but paddling like hell underneath.

—*Unknown*

1,030

Diner: What's the specialty of the house?
Waiter: The Heimlich maneuver.

—*Cartoon caption by Tom Meyer*

1,031

In some restaurants, the catch of the day is the waiter.

—*Phyllis Diller*

1,032

There is no politician in India daring enough to say that cows can be eaten.

—Indira Gandhi (1917–1984)

1,033

Sacred cows make the best hamburger.

—Mark Twain (1835–1910)

1,034

Hitler was a vegetarian.

—Sign in a San Francisco butcher shop

1,035

Revenge is sweet and not fattening.

—Alfred Hitchcock (1899–1980)

1,036

There is something soothing about a pumpkin.

—Terry Pimsleur, president of the International Pumpkin Association

1,037

For women, eating has taken on the sinful status once reserved for sex.

—*Unknown*

1,038

Whether or not one eats a cat is a personal choice.

—*Mike Royko (1932–1997)*

1,039

Breakfast cereals that come in the same colors as polyester leisure suits make oversleeping a virtue.

—*Fran Lebowitz*

1,040

Fettuccine Alfredo is macaroni and cheese for adults.

—*Mitch Hedberg (1968–2005)*

1,041

Sea World has a seafood restaurant. What do they serve, slow learners?

—*Lynda Montgomery*

1,042

If you don't find our canned corn beef to be all you hoped it would be, just leave word with the executor of your estate to return the unopened cans for a refund.

—*Bob Elliott (1922–1990) and Ray Goulding*

1,043

I've given up sex in favor of food. Now the mirrors are over the dining room table.

—*Phil Harris (1904–1995)*

1,044

More lousy dishes are presented under the banner of pâté than any other.

—*Kingsley Amis (1922–1995)*

1,045

I celebrated Thanksgiving the old-fashioned way. I invited the neighbors over for a huge feast, then I killed them and took their land.

—*Jon Stewart*

1,046

Once at Phillips Exeter Academy a student was hit in the face by a piece of dining-hall meat loaf. Some of it got in his mouth and he died.

—*P. J. O'Rourke*

1,047

My mother is such a lousy cook that Thanksgiving at her house is a time of sorrow.

—*Rita Rudner*

1,048

My cooking is so bad I have an oven that flushes.

—*Phyllis Diller*

1,049

My wife treads a fine line between cooking and arson.

—*Bill Hoest (*The Lockhorns*) (1926–1988)*

1,050

When you burn the food, admit it. Don't blame it on global warming.

—*Bill Hoest,* The Lockhorns *(1926–1988)*

1,051

Never order barbecue in a place that also serves quiche.

—*Lewis Grizzard (1946–1994)*

1,052

Never eat Chinese food in Oklahoma.

—*Bryan Miller*

1,053

Give me a dozen heartbreaks if they would help me lose a few pounds.

—*Colette (1873–1954)*

1,054

Cooking tip: wrap turkey leftovers in aluminum foil and throw them out.

—*Nicole Hollander*

1,055

On Thanksgiving, my mom, after six Bloody Marys, looks at the turkey and says, "Here, kitty, kitty."

—*David Letterman*

1,056

Gluttony is a sign that something is eating us.

—Peter De Vries (1910–1993)

1,057

Rice is great if you're really hungry and want to eat two thousand of something.

—Mitch Hedberg (1968–2005)

1,058

Food has replaced sex for many people. Now they can't even get into their *own* pants.

—Unknown

1,059

My diet is very effective. I eat only with naked fat people.

—Ed Bluestone

1,060

No one cries over spilt milk who is lactose intolerant.

—Chet Hurley

1,061

I went to a conference of bulimics and anorexics. It was horrible. The bulimics ate the anorexics.

—*Monica Piper*

1,062

The best time to eat Hot Pockets is when you are already sitting on the toilet.

—*Jim Gaffigan*

1,063

Vegetables are interesting but lack a sense of purpose when unaccompanied by a good cut of meat.

—*Fran Lebowitz*

1,064

Food gives meaning to dining-room furniture.

—*Fran Lebowitz*

1,065

Cannibals don't eat clowns because they taste funny.

—*Unknown*

1,066

People will eat anything if it is cut into small enough pieces.

—Leonard Powell

1,067

Canada is a country without a cuisine. When's the last time you went out for Canadian?

—Mike Myers

1,068

Great restaurants are mouth brothels. There is no point going to them if you intend to keep your belt buckled.

—Frederic Raphael

1,069

Do illiterate people get the full effect of alphabet soup?

—John Mendoza

1,070

Why go on a picnic when you can get the same effect by putting potato salad under a heat lamp?

—Maxine, the Crabby Lady (John Wagner)

1,071

I'm not overweight, I'm nine inches too short.

—*Shelley Winters (1920–2006)*

1,072

Fast food has destroyed more men than fast women.

—*Jim Murray (1919–1998)*

1,073

When men stay overnight, they want strange things for breakfast, like toast. I don't have those recipes.

—*Elayne Boosler*

1,074

The guy who invented headcheese must have been really hungry.

—*Jerry Seinfeld*

1,075

Never eat under an electric bug zapper.

—*From* Men's Health *magazine, 2003*

1,076

Man does not live by words alone, even though he sometimes has to eat them.

—*Adlai Stevenson (1900–1965)*

1,077

In Tulsa, restaurants have signs that say SORRY, WE'RE OPEN.

—*Roseanne Barr*

1,078

Family dinners are often an ordeal of nervous indigestion preceded by hidden resentment and ennui and accompanied by psychosomatic jitters.

—*M. F. K. Fisher (1908–1992)*

1,079

A friend asked me if I wanted a frozen banana. I said, "No, but I want a regular banana later, so . . . yeah."

—*Mitch Hedberg (1968–2005)*

1,080

A can that says Pepsi Free must have no Pepsi in it. So it's a Coke.

—*Gallagher*

1,081

Never eat anything that comes when you call.

—*Robert "Bobcat" Goldthwait*

1,082

The most dangerous food is the wedding cake.

—*James Thurber (1894–1961)*

1,083

I don't like coffee, but neither do I like it when I fall asleep and my head hits the desk.

—*Brian Andreas*

1,084

If I can't have too many truffles, I'll do without.

—*Colette (1873–1954)*

1,085

I started a grease fire at McDonald's by throwing a match in the cook's hair.

—Steve Martin

1,086

Search parties are sent out for fat people first, because when slim people are missing, everybody assumes they simply got a better offer.

—Garrison Keillor

1,087

You can save money with smaller portions, which is why I restrict myself to just one woman.

—Leo Roberts

1,088

Give a man food and he can eat for a day; give him a job and he will get between thirty and sixty minutes to eat.

—Lev L. Spiro

1,089

My doctor told me to stop having intimate dinners for four unless there are three other people.

—Orson Welles (1915–1985)

1,090

My friends tell me that cooking is easy, but it's not easier than not cooking.

—*Maria Bamford*

1,091

Lots of people think you shouldn't eat before going to bed at night. Then why is there a light in the refrigerator?

—*Deon Cole*

1,092

Blimpie supplies sandwiches to Delta Airlines to serve on its flights. In return, Delta gives Blimpie barf bags for its restaurants.

—*Norm Macdonald*

1,093

Most plants taste better when they've had to suffer a little.

—*Diana Kennedy*

1,094

Cotton candy is just sugar made to look like insulation.

—*Mike Birbiglia*

DRINK

1,095

Drunkenness is voluntary insanity.

—*Seneca (4 BC–AD 65)*

1,096

I was so drunk last night I fell down and missed the floor.

—*Harry Crane*

1,097

I got so drunk one night I woke up in a chalk outline.

—*Tim Northern*

1,098

I cook with wine. Sometimes I add it to the food.

—*Robert Morley (1908–1992)*

1,099

A drunk would not give money to sober people because they would only buy food and clothes with it and send their children to school.

—*Samuel Butler (1835–1902)*

1,100

If you drink like a fish, swim, don't drive.

—*Unknown*

1,101

Water taken in moderation cannot hurt anybody.

—*Mark Twain (1835–1910)*

1,102

Love makes the world go round, but whiskey makes it go round twice as fast.

—*Compton McKenzie*

1,103

I come from a long line of alcoholics. My family tree has a car wrapped around it.

—*Mike Lawren*

1,104

I distrust camels and anybody else who can go a week without a drink.

—*Joe E. Lewis (1902–1971)*

1,105

Whiskey is a torchlight procession down your throat.

—*John L. O'Sullivan (1813–1895)*

1,106

It is as easy to get drunk on water as it is on land.

—*George Gobel (1919–1991)*

1,107

One tequila, two tequila, three tequila, floor.

—*George Carlin (1937–2008)*

1,108

Alcohol may be man's worst enemy, but the Bible says love your enemy.

—*Frank Sinatra (1915–1998)*

1,109

Alcohol is a good preservative for everything but brains.

—*Mary Pettibone Poole in* A Glass Eye at a Keyhole *(1938)*

1,110

There's nothing wrong with sobriety in moderation.

—*John Ciardi (1916–1986)*

1,111

The month of March is God's way of showing nondrinkers what a hangover is like.

—*Garrison Keillor*

1,112

His mouth had been used as a latrine by some small animal of the night.

—*Kingsley Amis (1922–1995), describing a hangover*

1,113

I'm as drunk as a lord, but then I am one, so what does it matter?

—*Lord Bertrand Russell (1872–1970)*

1,114

There are more old drunks than old doctors.

—*Unknown*

1,115

Socrates had a drinking problem.

—*Bob Ingram*

1,116

I collect bottles, which sounds better than "alcoholic."

—*Stewart Francis*

1,117

Scientists report that drinking beer can be good for the liver. I'm sorry, did I say "scientists"? I meant Irish people.

—*Tina Fey*

1,118

An alcoholic is someone you don't like who drinks as much as you do.

—*Brendan Behan (1923–1964)*

1,119

What is it about a beautiful, sunny afternoon with the birds singing and the wind rustling the leaves that makes you want to get drunk?

—*Jack Handey*

1,120

Betty Ford saw me naked and started drinking again.

—*Joan Rivers*

1,121

All vodka corrupts. Absolut vodka corrupts absolutely.

—*Stefan Kanfer*

1,122

There is a time for Buddhist meditation and there is a time for Irish whiskey.

—*Joseph Campbell (1904–1987)*

1,123

My favorite drink is a cocktail of carrot juice and whiskey. When I'm drunk, I can see for miles.

—*Roy Brown*

1,124

I finally met a woman who said the six words I've been waiting all my life to hear: "My dad owns a liquor store."

—*Mark Klein*

1,125

Researchers have developed a "red wine pill" that gives all the benefits of red wine without the alcohol. It's called a grape.

—*Norm Macdonald*

1,126

Beer is proof that God loves us and wants us to be happy.

—Benjamin Franklin (1706–1790)

1,127

I left my apartment to get some Snapple and a guy asked me if I wanted to buy some heroin. I said, "No. Got any Snapple?"

—Mike Birbiglia

HEALTH

1,128

Ever notice that fifteen minutes into a Jerry Lewis telethon you start rooting for the disease?

—Jim Sherbert

1,129

I was depressed all morning. Then a friend called and said she lost her job and her husband, and that made me feel a little better.

—Amy Foster

1,130

To cure seasickness, sit under a tree.

—Spike Milligan (1918–2002)

1,131

I recently became a Christian Scientist. It was the only health plan I could afford.

—Betsy Salkind

1,132

I've been straight for seventeen days . . . but not all in a row.

—*Sam Kinison (1953–1992)*

1,133

The entire economy of the Western world is built on things that cause cancer.

—*From the movie* Bliss, *1985*

1,134

Virus check completed. All viruses functioning normally.

—*Unknown*

1,135

I want all hellions to quit puffing that hell fume into God's clean air.

—*Carry Nation (1846–1911), on smoking*

1,136

Asthma bothers me if I'm around dogs or cigars. The worst are dogs smoking cigars.

—*Steve Allen (1921–2000)*

1,137

Smoking is much more enjoyable around nonsmokers.

—Dr. Bob Ben

1,138

I smoke Raleighs because with fifty thousand coupons they give you a brass coffin.

—Earl Weaver

1,139

Cancer? Perhaps. Flavor? For sure!

—Cigarette ad in the movie Crazy People, *1990*

1,140

A person's right to smoke ends where the next person's nose begins.

—*Unknown*

1,141

I smoke cigars. I don't like the flavor, but I enjoy the privacy.

—*Rick Corso*

1,142

Smoking knocks ten years off your life, but it's the last ten. So what will you miss, the drooling?

—*John Mendoza*

1,143

If you laid all the smokers end to end around the world, 67 percent of them would drown.

—*Steve Altman*

1,144

In hospitals there is no time off for good behavior.

—*Josephine Tey (1896–1952)*

1,145

If everyone took tranquilizers, nobody would need them.

—*Edmund Orrin*

1,146

I love my friends. Without them I'd be the most screwed-up person I know.

—*Margot Black*

1,147

I drive much too fast to worry about cholesterol.

—*Steven Wright*

1,148

If you have a headache, do what it says on the aspirin bottle: "Take two aspirin" and "Keep away from children."

—*Unknown*

1,149

Therapy is like going to grad school and majoring in yourself.

—*Fran Drescher*

1,150

It's hard to be nice to some paranoid schizophrenic just because she lives in your body.

—*Judy Tenuta*

1,151

Sanity is a cozy lie.

—*Susan Sontag (1933–2004)*

1,152

I used to do drugs. I still do, but I used to, too.

—*Mitch Hedberg (1968–2005)*

1,153

Comedy has always been in my blood. The hepatitis is new.

—*Tom Cotter*

1,154

Among the many remedies that won't cure a cold, the most common is advice.

—*Unknown*

1,155

Whiskey is the most popular of the remedies that won't cure a cold.

—*Jerry Vale*

1,156

Salmonella is a bacterium that in the human bloodstream can grow into an adult salmon.

—*Dave Barry*

1,157

Doctors have identified a new disfiguring disease called the DMV syndrome. Victims look like their driver's license photos.

—Nick at Night

1,158

I sneezed a sneeze into the air;
It fell to earth I know not where.
You should have seen the looks on those
In whose vicinity I snoze.

—*Ish Kabibble (Merwyn Bogue, 1908–1994)*

1,159

Laughter is the best medicine—unless you're diabetic, then insulin is the best.

—*Jasper Carrott*

1,160

In the hospital waiting room I saw a dozen people holding urine samples. It was like being at a Snapple convention.

—*Nick Di Paolo*

1,161

I'm not opposed to all drugs. I watch TV.

—*Paul Krassner*

1,162

When doctors find something in your bladder, it's never anything good, like tickets to a Yankees game.

—*Mike Birbiglia*

1,163

I have flabby thighs, but fortunately my stomach covers them.

—*Joan Rivers*

1,164

I'll consider jogging if I ever see a jogger smiling.

—*Joan Rivers*

1,165

Walking like a dork is popular among people who used to jog for their health but who can no longer afford orthopedic surgery.

—*Dave Barry*

1,166

The only exercise I have time for is a run in my stockings.

—*Donna Gephart*

1,167

For exercise, I stumble and fall into a coma.

—*Oscar Levant (1906–1972)*

1,168

The word *aerobics* came about when gym instructors realized that they couldn't charge $15 an hour for it if they called it "jumping up and down."

—*Rita Rudner*

1,169

The ultimate indignity is to be given a bedpan by a stranger who calls you by your first name.

—*Maggie Kuhn (1905–1995)*

1,170

When I don't feel like going to the gynecologist, I phone him, snap on the rubber gloves, and ask him to walk me through it.

—*Dame Edna Everage (Barry Humphries)*

1,171

Seven out of ten people suffer from hemorrhoids. Do the other three enjoy them?

—*Sal Davino*

1,172

I'm sick of hearing about twelve-step programs for changing behavior. What we need are fewer twelve-step programs and more twelve-gauge shotguns.

—*Name withheld by request*

1,173

We need a twelve-step program for compulsive talkers. It would be called On Anon Anon.

—*Paula Poundstone*

1,174

At Overachievers Anonymous there are twenty-four steps.

—*Unknown*

1,175

I don't jog. It makes the ice jump right out of my glass.

—*Martin Mull*

1,176

I'm very health conscious. I'm in terrible shape, but I'm aware of it.

—*Stevie Ray Fromstein*

1,177

I exercise in the morning before my brain figures out what I'm doing.

—Marsha Doble

1,178

The only time I run is when the ice-cream truck is doing sixty.

—Wendy Liebman

1,179

If you ever see me jogging, tell the bus driver that my arm is caught in the door.

—Jeff Shaw

1,180

I'd do anything for a good body except diet and exercise.

—Steve Martin

1,181

I had a lazy eye as a kid and it gradually spread to my whole body.

—Tom Cotter

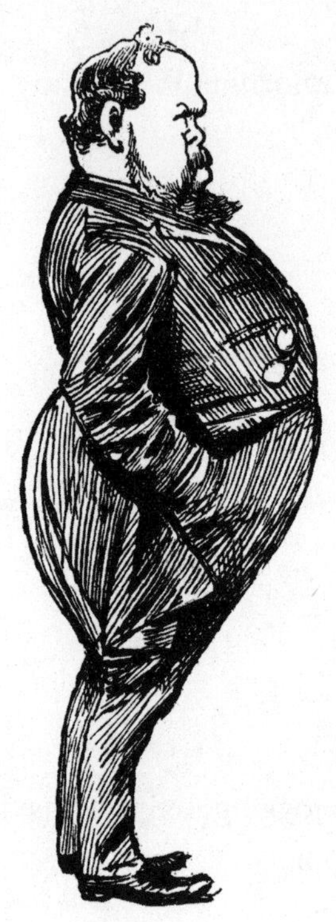

1,182

I was told to listen to my body when jogging. My body said, "What are you doing? Are you crazy? Sit down!"

—*Chet Hurley*

1,183

I don't work out. My philosophy is "No pain, no pain."

—*Carol Leifer*

1,184

Muscles come and go; flab stays.

—*Bill Vaughan (1915–1977)*

1,185

The abdomen is a cavity containing the organs of indigestion.

—*Evan Esar (1899–1995)*

1,186

Some people exercise by jumping to conclusions, others by sidestepping their responsibilities, but most people by running down their friends.

—*Evan Esar (1899–1995)*

1,187

A tennis ball is worse than a tennis elbow.

—*John Burkhart (1928–2010)*

1,188

A nervous breakdown shows you care.

—*Robert Orben*

1,189

Just before somebody gets nervous, do they get cocoons in the stomach?

—*Unknown*

1,190

She's so anally retentive she's afraid to sit down for fear of sucking up the furniture.

—*Jennifer Saunders*

1,191

Dad always thought that laughter was the best medicine, which I guess is why so many of us died of tuberculosis.

—*Jack Handey*

1,192

When standing next to a tall person, a short person can easily have a stature-impairment episode.

—*Unknown*

1,193

Inside every short person is a tall person doubled over in pain.

—*Jeremy Kramer*

1,194

I've just learned about his illness. Let's hope it's nothing trivial.

—Irwin S. Cobb (1876–1944)

1,195

I finally have a dental plan. I chew on the other side.

—Janine Ditullio

1,196

Being Canadian, Jewish, and a writer, I have impeccable paranoia credentials.

—Mordecai Richler (1931–2001)

1,197

Miracles occur in psychoanalysis as seldom as anywhere else.

—Karen Horney (1885–1952), psychiatrist

1,198

In the health-care area, Republicans have unveiled their "Get Tough on Sick People" policy.

—Stephen Colbert

1,199

Republicans have a two-pronged plan for health care for the poor. Prong one is don't get sick. Prong two is don't get poor.

—Steve Bridges as Barack Obama

1,200

Resentment is like drinking poison and waiting for the other person to die.

—Carrie Fisher

1,201

I envy paranoids; they actually think that people are paying attention to them.

—Susan Sontag (1933–2004)

1,202

Sometimes I feel that the whole world is against me, but I know that's not true. Some countries are neutral.

—Robert Orben

DOCTORS

1,203

The practice of medicine today is so specialized that each doctor is a healer of one disease and no more.

—Herodotus (circa 430 BC)

1,204

A doctor's reputation is made by the number of eminent men who die under his care.

—George Bernard Shaw (1856–1950)

1,205

When my dad went to work during the dermatologists' strike, people shouted, "Scab!"

—Harry Hill

1,206

The doctor must have given me a faulty pacemaker. When my husband kisses me the garage door goes up.

—Minnie Pearl (1912–1996)

1,207

Only a doctor can ask a woman to undress and then send a bill to her husband.

—Jackie Mason

1,208

First, the doctor told me the good news. He said that I was going to have a disease named after me.

—Steve Martin

1,209

My doctor always washes his hands before touching my wallet.

—Joey Adams (1911–1999)

1,210

Orthodox medicine has not found an answer to your complaint. However, luckily for you, I happen to be a quack.

—Cartoon caption by Mischa Richter (1910–1992)

1,211

My husband was so ugly he was hired to stand outside his doctor's office to make people sick.

—Jackie "Moms" Mabley (1894–1975)

1,212

The way to a man's heart is through his aorta.

—Jerome Manheim, MD

1,213

The way to a man's heart is through his stomach . . . just be sure to thrust upward through the rib cage.

—Stephen Colbert

1,214

A friend of mine went to a doctor for a ringing in his ear. The doctor gave him an unlisted ear.

—Charlie Callas (1927–2011)

1,215

Doctors and nurses are people who give you medicine until you die.

—Deborah Martin

1,216

Half of modern drugs could be thrown out the window, but then the birds might eat them.

—Dr. Martin H. Fischer (1879–1962)

1,217

One of the best-kept medical secrets is that everything gives mice cancer.

—Marvin Kitman

1,218

The difference between doctors and lawyers is that lawyers merely rob you, while doctors rob you and kill you, too.

—Anton Chekhov (1860–1904), who was a doctor

1,219

Doctor to patient: "You're fifty-seven years old. I'd like to get that down a bit."

—Cartoon caption by Leo Cullum (1942–2010)

1,220

People with beepers are either doctors or drug dealers, if there is a distinction.

—Michael Feldman

1,221

It is no measure of health to be well adjusted to a sick society.

—*Jiddu Krishnamurti (1895–1986)*

1,222

Is there a doctor in the house? My mother wants me to marry you.

—*Wendy Liebman*

1,223

Doctor, when will my husband be well enough to sit up and take criticism?

—*Cartoon caption by Chon Day (1907–2000)*

1,224

I was going to have plastic surgery until I noticed that the doctor's office was full of portraits by Picasso.

—*Rita Rudner*

1,225

Psychoanalysis is a process that usually takes years, which is why Freudians have such lovely summer homes.

—*Cynthia Heimel*

1,226

Sigmund Freud and Carl Jung split over penis envy. Freud thought that every woman wanted a penis, while Jung thought every woman wanted *his* penis.

—*Ellen Orchid*

1,227

When I told my psychiatrist that nobody listened to me, he shouted, "Next!"

—*Henry "Henny" Youngman (1906–1998)*

AGING

1,228

Middle age is such a nice change from being young.

—Dorothy Canfield Fisher (1879–1958)

1,229

You're only young once, but you can be immature forever.

—Germaine Greer

1,230

Middle age is having a choice of temptations and choosing the one that will get you home earlier.

—Dan Bennett

1,231

Middle age is when a narrow waist and a broad mind begin to change places.

—Glenn Dorenbush (1930–1966)

1,232

It's hard to accept that you've always been a nobody and that you'll never be as important again.

—*Harry F. Noyes III*

1,233

The lovely thing about being forty is that you appreciate twenty-five-year-old men more.

—*Colleen McCullough*

1,234

I believe that everybody my age is an adult, while I am merely in disguise.

—*Margaret Atwood*

1,235

As you get older, the pickings get slimmer, but the people don't.

—*Carrie Fisher*

1,236

My husband will never chase another woman. He's too fine, he's too decent, he's too old.

—*Gracie Allen (1895–1964) in 1960, when George Burns (1896–1996) was only sixty-four*

1,237

At age eighty-two, I sometimes feel like a twenty-year-old, but there's seldom one around.

—Milton Berle (1908–2002)

1,238

You know you're old when somebody compliments you on your alligator shoes and you're barefoot.

—Phyllis Diller

1,239

There are no old people anymore. They are either "wonderful for their age" or dead.

—Mary Pettibone Poole (dates unknown)

1,240

At my age, flowers scare me.

—George Burns (1896–1996)

1,241

Age doesn't matter, unless you're a cheese.

—Billie Burke (1884–1970)

1,242

I refuse to admit that I'm older than fifty-two, even if that makes my sons illegitimate.

—Lady Nancy Astor (1879–1964)

1,243

The older one grows, the more one likes indecency.

—Virginia Woolf (1882–1941)

1,244

Be nice to your children, for they will choose your rest home.

—*Phyllis Diller*

1,245

I don't have any secrets. I just forget a lot of stuff.

—*Brian Andreas*

1,246

It's hard to be nostalgic when you can't remember anything.

—*Unknown*

1,247

Nostalgia is like a grammar lesson where you find the present tense and the past perfect.

—*Unknown*

1,248

I hate nostalgia. Hated it then and hate it now.

—*Ed Asner*

1,249

I'll never make the mistake of being seventy again.

—*Casey Stengel (1890–1975)*

1,250

Growing old is like being increasingly punished for a crime you didn't commit.

—*Anthony Powell (1905–2000)*

1,251

Age is a high price to pay for maturity.

—*Tom Stoppard*

1,252

I know the secret of Dick Clark's youthful looks. In 1956 he had himself laminated.

—*Johnny Carson (1925–2005)*

1,253

No man knows what true happiness is until he has a complete set of false teeth and has lost all interest in the opposite sex.

—*Lord Rosbery (1847–1929)*

1,254

I'm so old bartenders check my pulse instead of my ID.

—*Louise Bowie*

1,255

The aging process could be slowed down if it had to work its way through Congress.

—*George H. W. Bush*

1,256

One of the delights known to age and beyond the grasp of youth is that of Not Going.

—*Anthony Burgess (1917–1993)*

1,257

As an old person, I begin each day with coffee and obituaries.

—*Bill Cosby*

1,258

Memory is like a crazy old woman who hoards colored rags and throws away food.

—*Dr. Austin O'Malley (1858–1932)*

1,259

My mother is in a retirement home for women that is entirely powered by hot flashes.

—*Chet Hurley*

1,260

My parents have retired to a little death-and-breakfast place in Florida.

—*Richard Lewis*

1,261

In India, the life expectancy is thirty-nine, but cows live into their eighties.

—*Charles Bragg*

1,262

In a dream you are never eighty.

—*Anne Sexton (1928–1974)*

1,263

Dying would wreck my image.

—*Fitness guru Jack LaLanne (1914–2011), at age ninety-five*

1,264

When I was a boy, the Dead Sea was only sick.

—*George Burns (1896–1996)*

1,265

The British House of Lords is a model of how to care for the elderly.

—*Frank Field*

1,266

My grandmother took a speed-weeping course.

—*Richard Lewis*

1,267

Early to bed and early to rise
Makes a man wish for his demise.

—*Darrin Weinberg*

1,268

When I was young I wanted a BMW. Now I don't care about the *W*.

—*Unknown*

1,269

Maturity has a lot going for it. For example, you no longer get bubble gum stuck in your braces.

—*Cyra McFadden*

1,270

At my age I don't need drugs anymore. I can get the same effect by standing up real fast.

—*Jonathan Katz*

1,271

I'm now at an age where I have to prove that I'm as good as I never was.

—*Rex Harrison (1908–1990)*

1,272

The older one becomes, the quicker the present fades into sepia and the past looms up in glorious Technicolor.

—*Beryl Bainbridge (1932–2010)*

1,273

My memory is not as sharp as it used to be. Also, my memory is not as sharp as it used to be.

—*Maxine, the Crabby Lady (John Wagner)*

1,274

You're not young anymore when you are obsessed with the thermostat.

—*Jeff Foxworthy*

1,275

Old people are fond of giving advice; it consoles them for no longer being capable of setting bad examples.

—*François La Rochefoucauld (1613–1680)*

1,276

Never trust anyone under eighty.

—*Carol Brightman*

SUICIDE

1,277

I was going to commit suicide by sticking my head in the oven, but there was a cake in it.

—*Lesley Boone*

1,278

Always carry a gun. Not to shoot yourself but to know that you are always making a choice.

—*Lisa Wertmuller*

1,279

Never murder a man who is committing suicide.

—*Woodrow Wilson (1856–1924)*

1,280

If somebody with a split personality threatens to kill himself, is that a hostage situation?

—*George Carlin (1937–2008)*

1,281

There are those who dare not kill themselves for fear of what the neighbors will say.

—Cyril Connolly (1903–1974)

1,282

Suicide is the sincerest form of self-criticism.

—Unknown

1,283

A lack of accuracy can be an advantage if you're hurling yourself on your sword.

—Chet Hurley

1,284

Doctor to wife of patient: "Before we suggest assisted suicide to your husband, Mrs. Rose, let's give the aspirin a chance to work."

—Cartoonist Walt Handelsman

1,285

I haven't decided yet about assisted suicide. I'm still working on assisted homicide.

—Dr. Thomas Eisner (1929–2011)

1,286

Drink and sex are what killed my uncle. He couldn't get either so he shot himself.

—*From* The Benny Hill Show, *1969*

1,287

Suicide is a way of saying to God, "You can't fire me! I quit!"

—*Bill Maher*

1,288

I tried to hang myself with a bungee cord. I kept almost killing myself.

—*Steven Wright*

1,289

Books on suicide can be found in the self-help section.

—*Bob Newhart*

1,290

I couldn't commit suicide if my life depended on it.

—*George Carlin (1937–2008)*

1,291

A suicide note written by somebody who isn't suicidal is called an autobiography.

—Dane Cook

1,292

You can't get books on suicide at the library because people don't return them.

—Kevin Nealon

1,293

A suicide hotline is where they talk to you until you don't feel like killing yourself. Exactly the opposite of a call from a telemarketer.

—Dana Snow

1,294

My wife made me join a bridge club. I jump off next Tuesday.

—Rodney Dangerfield (1921–2004)

DEATH

1,295

Being a living legend is better than being a dead legend.

—George Burns (1896–1996)

1,296

Some people are alive because it is against the law to kill them.

—Edgar Watson Howe (1853–1937)

1,297

I have never killed a man, but I have read many obituaries with pleasure.

—Clarence Darrow (1857–1938)

1,298

Always remember the last words of my grandfather, who said, "A truck!"

—Emo Philips

1,299

Death is nature's way of telling you to slow down.

—Newsweek, *April 25, 1960*

1,300

Where there's a will, there's a relative.

—Ricky Gervais

1,301

Let us live in a way so that when we die, even the undertaker will be sorry.

—Mark Twain (1835–1910)

1,302

I suffer from reincarnation anxiety. I'm afraid I'll come back as myself.

—Richard Lewis

1,303

I intend to live forever. So far, so good.

—Steven Wright

1,304

For Truman Capote (1924–1984), dying was a good career move.

—*Gore Vidal*

1,305

You don't die of a broken heart; you only wish you did.

—*Marilyn Peterson*

1,306

Life is pleasant. Death is peaceful. It's the transition that's troublesome.

—*Isaac Asimov (1920–1992)*

1,307

What I look forward to is continued immaturity followed by death.

—*Dave Barry*

1,308

Death is an effective way of cutting down on your expenses.

—*Woody Allen*

1,309

If Einstein couldn't beat death, what chance do I have?

—Mel Brooks

1,310

If Abraham Lincoln were alive today, he'd be clawing at the inside of his coffin.

—David Letterman

1,311

You don't get to choose how you're going to die, only how you're going to live.

—Joan Baez

1,312

Consider the case of Father La Tour, a priest who went to Lourdes for his asthma and died of a heart attack.

—Charles Bragg

1,313

Life is tough. Three out of four people die.

—Ring Lardner (1885–1933)

1,314

I would never die for my beliefs because I might be wrong.

—Bertrand Russell (1872–1970)

1,315

My husband, Norm, died after spending years in a hospital suffering from a testicular murmur. He donated all of his organs, leaving behind only a dent in his pillow.

—Dame Edna Everage (Barry Humphries)

1,316

I didn't attend the funeral, but I sent a nice letter saying I approved of it.

—Mark Twain (1835–1910)

1,317

No matter how important you are, the size of your funeral will depend on the weather.

—Roger Miller (1936–1992)

1,318

Don't hang him in effigy, hang him right here in Boston.

—From the TV series Cheers

1,319

Everything is drive-through in California. There's a burial service called Jump-in-the-Box.

—*Wil Shriner*

1,320

The living are the dead on vacation.

—*Maurice de Maeterlinck (1862–1949)*

1,321

I have one last request. Don't use embalming fluid on me. I want to be stuffed with crabmeat.

—*Woody Allen*

1,322

He's one tough cookie. I've never seen anyone bounce back from an autopsy before.

—*Cartoonist Mike Twohy*

1,323

When I die, I want my crotch cremated and the ashes spread over the Virgin Islands.

—*Bruce Baum*

1,324

Good health is the slowest rate at which you can die.

—*Unknown*

1,325

When I die, I'm going to leave my body to science fiction.

—*Steven Wright*

1,326

If I were God, I'd abolish death . . . but not for everybody.

—*Cynthia Ozick*

1,327

Death is the sound of distant thunder at a picnic.

—*W. H. Auden (1907–1973)*

1,328

The worst time to have a heart attack is during a game of charades.

—*Demetri Martin*

1,329

If you die in an elevator, be sure to push the "up" button.

—*Sam Levenson (1911–1980)*

1,330

There is a report that Piso is dead. He was an honest man, intelligent and agreeable, generous and faithful, provided he is really dead.

—*Jean de la Bruyère (1645–1696)*

1,331

When you have told anyone you have left them a legacy, the only decent thing to do is die at once.

—*Samuel Butler (1835–1902)*

1,332

A worker at a tool-and-die factory died when he was hit by a tool.

—*George Carlin (1937–2008)*

1,333

I took my family to see *Disney on Ice*. All things considered, he looked pretty good.

—*Unknown*

1,334

My aunt passed away and was cremated. We think that's what did it.

—*Jonathan Katz*

1,335

Canadians are cold so much of the time most of them choose cremation.

—*Cynthia Nelms*

1,336

Always read books that will make you look good if you die in the middle of them.

—*P. J. O'Rourke*

1,337

God invented rain to give dead people something to complain about.

—*David Brenner*

1,338

My grandmother spends all of her time in the garden because that's where she's buried.

—*Tom Cotter*

1,339

Doctor to patient: "You only have a week to live. Start taking mud baths to get used to dirt."

—Prairie Home Companion, *March 1999*

1,340

I told you I was ill!

—*What Spike Milligan (1918–2002) suggested for his tombstone*

1,341

Stay in touch, eh?

—*Epitaph on a Canadian tombstone*

1,342

My uncle was an angry man. On his tombstone it says WHAT ARE YOU LOOKING AT?

—*Mitch Hedberg (1968–2005)*

1,343

Wherever she went, including here, it was against her better judgment.

—*What Dorothy Parker (1893–1967) suggested for her tombstone*

1,344

This is on me.

—*Another suggestion by Dorothy Parker for her tombstone*

1,345

If tombstones told the truth, everybody would want to be buried at sea.

—John Raper

1,346

Here lies my wife; let her lie!
Now she's at rest, and so am I.

—John Dryden (1631–1700)

1,347

I want my tombstone to say FIGMENT.

—Andy Warhol (1928–1987)

1,348

Over my dead body!

—What Franklin P. Adams (1881–1960) suggested for his tombstone

1,349

We all have to die, I understand that, but why do we have to crawl to the finish line?

—Paula Poundstone

1,350

All work and no play makes Jack a dull boy and Jill a rich widow.

—Evan Esar (1899–1995)

1,351

An ounce of taffy is worth a pound of epitaphy.

—Fred Craddock

1,352

It takes Norwegians so long to die they have to start when they're young.

—Garrison Keillor

1,353

Now there are bereavement classes for women whose husbands won't die.

—Frank P. Barba

1,354

If I'm on life support, pull the plug when I get down to a size eight.

—Henrietta Montel

1,355

Maybe all one can do is hope to end up with the right regrets.

—Arthur Miller (1915–2005)

1,356

We will all die someday if we live long enough.

—Dave Farber

1,357

You shouldn't say anything about the dead unless it's good. He's dead. Good.

—Jackie "Moms" Mabley (1894–1975)

1,358

A friend said that in the next life she'd like to come back as a porcupine. She doesn't like crowds.

—Brian Andreas

1,359

God put me on this earth to accomplish a certain number of things. I'm so far behind I will never die.

—*Bill Watterson*

1,360

Rejected names for nursing homes:

Trail's End
Final Sunset
The Pulled Plug
Whispering Pines Storage Locker

—*Leo Roberts*

SHOW BUSINESS

1,361

I've never made *Who's Who*, but I'm featured in *What's That?*

—Phyllis Diller

1,362

If life was fair, Elvis would be alive and all the impersonators would be dead.

—Johnny Carson (1927–2005)

1,363

The worldwide slobbering over celebrities, often by those who became celebrities by slobbering over celebrities, is a crime against journalism.

—Walter Goodman (1927–2002)

1,364

I don't mind being called a dumb blonde because I know I'm not dumb and I know I'm not blond.

—*Dolly Parton*

1,365

I signed my likeness away to help publicize *Star Wars*. Now every time I look in the mirror, I have to send George Lucas a couple of bucks.

—*Carrie Fisher recalling her role in* Star Wars

1,366

To be a celebrity in America is to be forgiven everything.

—*Mary McGrory (1918–2004)*

1,367

A celebrity is someone who looks as if he spent more than two hours on his hair.

—*Steve Martin*

1,368

Because of web pages, everyone on earth will soon have fifteen megabytes of fame.

—*M. G. Siriam*

1,369

Hollywood is the only place where you can wake up and hear the birds coughing in the trees.

—Joe Frisco (1889–1958)

1,370

I first billed myself as a singer from Rhode Island, an act of Providence.

—George Burns (1896–1996)

1,371

The world's only one-word oxymoron: Madonna.

—John Tigges (1932–2008)

1,372

I hate parties. Why should I decorate somebody else's room?

—Lauren Bacall

1,373

Acting is the art of keeping a large group of people from coughing.

—Ralph Richardson (1902–1983)

1,374

Cher looks good but embalmed.

—Rebecca Christian

1,375

Researchers have developed a self-healing plastic that will repair itself if cracked. In a related story, Joan Rivers will never die.

—Tina Fey

1,376

In Hollywood, if you die from too much plastic surgery and liposuction, it's called natural causes.

—Bill Maher

1,377

One measure of success is the number of things written about you that aren't true.

—Cybill Shepherd

1,378

My fan club has finally disbanded. The guy died.

—Phyllis Diller

1,379

You can calculate Zsa Zsa Gabor's age by counting the rings on her fingers.

—*Bob Hope (1903–2003)*

1,380

Publicity is like poison. It only hurts you if you swallow it.

—*Sam Rutigliano*

1,381

A popular Halloween mask is Arnold Schwarzenegger. With their mouths full of candy, children sound just like him.

—*Conan O'Brien*

1,382

If you are famous, eventually some very nice people will give you a doctorate in fine arts for doing jack squat.

—*Stephen Colbert*

1,383

Fame means that millions of people have the wrong idea of who you are.

—*Erica Jong*

1,384

Comedian Judy Tenuta is actually a caring nurturer who wakes up at 8:00 p.m. to verbally abuse herds of mortal swine (her audiences) and converts them to her religion, Judyism.

—From her website, July 2011

1,385

When choosing a movie, the opinion of a dumb friend is better than the opinion of a smart critic.

—George Leonard (1923–2010)

1,386

The only ism Hollywood believes in is plagiarism.

—Dorothy Parker (1893–1967)

1,387

The definition of "crazy" in Hollywood is a woman who keeps talking even after nobody wants to sleep with her anymore.

—Tina Fey

1,388

After watching a documentary, I often end up hating a whole new group of people.

—Bryce Parks

1,389

Her only flair is in her nostrils.

—Movie critic Pauline Kael (1919–2001) about an actress

1,390

In Hollywood, it is considered bad manners to stab somebody in the chest.

—Julia Phillips (1944–2002)

1,391

Acting is hell. You spend all your time trying to do what they put people in asylums for.

—Jane Fonda

1,392

When it comes to movie ratings, G means the good guy gets the girl, R means the bad guy gets the girl, and X means everybody gets the girl.

—Kirk Douglas

1,393

If I had known what a big shot Michael was going to become, I would have been nicer to him as a kid.

—Kirk Douglas

1,394

An actor is a guy who if you ain't talking about him ain't listening.

—Marlon Brando (1924–2004)

1,395

You can pick out the actors by the glazed look that comes into their eyes when the conversation wanders away from themselves.

—Michael Wilding (1912–1979)

1,396

Bad acting and bad dialogue make this a joy to watch.

—Michael Weldon in a review of the movie Jesse James Meets Frankenstein's Daughter

1,397

I'm not the public.

—Lauren Bacall on being told that a store was not open to the public

1,398

Don't judge a book by its movie.

—J. W. Eagan

1,399

Quitting acting is a sign of maturity.

—Marlon Brando (1924–2004)

1,400

I'm no actor and I have seventy movies to prove it.

—Victor Mature (1913–1999)

1,401

I'll just say what's in my heart: ba-bump, ba-bump, ba-bump.

—Mel Brooks accepting an Oscar for The Produers

1,402

On leaving the *Tonight* show, I was reminded of my mother's words when I left home as a young man: "How far do you think you'll get in that dress?"

—Johnny Carson (1925–2005)

1,403

Getting a movie made in Hollywood is like trying to grill a steak by having a succession of people coming into the room and breathing on it.

—Douglas Adams (1952–2001)

1,404

Being a writer in Hollywood is like going into Hitler's office with a great idea for a bar mitzvah.

—David Mamet

1,405

Shirley MacLaine could go to group therapy all by herself.

—Cynthia Nelms

1,406

I look like a rock quarry that someone has dynamited.

—Charles Bronson

1,407

Several tons of dynamite are set off in this movie, none of it under the right people.

—Movie review by James Agee (1909–1955)

1,408

I don't care what you say about me as long as you say something about me.

—George M. Cohan (1878–1942)

1,409

Being a star is not a profession. It's an accident.

—Lauren Bacall

1,410

Fredric March was able to do a very emotional scene with tears in his eyes and pinch my fanny at the same time.

—Shelley Winters (1920–2006)

1,411

I wouldn't consider dying during a newspaper strike.

—Bette Davis (1908–1989)

1,412

Success is a great deodorant.

—Elizabeth Taylor (1932–2011)

1,413

Success is having to worry about every damned thing in the world except money.

—Johnny Cash (1932–2003)

1,414

Science shows that fertility and movie offers drop off steeply for women after age forty.

—Tina Fey

1,415

Alfred Hitchcock is a gentleman farmer who raises goose-flesh.

—Ingrid Bergman (1915–1982)

1,416

The words Kiss Kiss Bang Bang, which I once saw on an Italian poster, are perhaps the briefest statement imaginable of the basic appeal of movies.

—Pauline Kael (1919–2001)

1,417

The play had only one fault. It was kind of lousy.

—James Thurber (1894–1961)

1,418

You can't tell a book from its movie.

—*Louis A. Safian*

1,419

Why don't they just get taller girls?

—*Fred Allen (1894–1956) at the ballet*

1,420

Male ballet dancers wear pants so tight you can tell what religion they are.

—*Robin Williams*

1,421

I could dance with you till the cows come home, but I'd rather dance with the cows till you come home.

—*Groucho Marx (1890–1977)*

1,422

Cosmetic surgery is so common in Hollywood that people now ask, "Is that your real head?"

—*Sue Kolinsky*

1,423

You remind me of my brother, but he has a human head.

—*Judy Tenuta*

MUSIC

1,424

Without music, life would be a mistake.

—*Friedrich Nietzsche (1844–1900)*

1,425

Country song titles:

Life Is Like Nebraska Without You (David Lott)

I Know Why the Caged Bird Stinks (Robert Byrne)

Ain't No Trash Been in My Trailer Since the Night I Threw You Out (Paul Hemmer)

I've Enjoyed as Much of You as I Can Stand (Bill Anderson)

You Just Sorta Stomped on My Aorta (lyrics by John Denver)

I'd Shoot You 'Cause You Stole My Heart, but You Stole My Gun as Well (Ellen Schisle)

1,426

More country song titles:

Your Wife Is Cheatin' on Us Again (Kemp and Robb)

I Asked Her Not to Break My Heart so She Broke My Collarbone (Walt Garrison)

I Ain't Got but One Nerve Left, and You've Done Got on That (Richard Northcutt)

When You Kicked Me in the Teeth You Hurt My Fillings (Jack Labow)

I Lost My Love for Gina When She Served Me a Subpoena (Robert Byrne)

Since the Night You Flew the Coop, My Cock Has Crowed Alone (Leo Roberts)

1,427

I don't like country music, but I don't mean to denigrate those who do. If you like it, *denigrate* means "to put down."

—*Bob Newhart*

1,428

Brass bands are all very well in their place—outdoors and several miles away.

—*Sir Thomas Beecham (1879–1961)*

1,429

Too many pieces of music finish too long after the end.

—Igor Stravinsky (1882–1971)

1,430

There is no female Mozart for the same reason there is no female Jack the Ripper.

—Camille Paglia

1,431

The guitar is all right, but you'll never make a living at it.

—John Lennon's aunt Mimi (John Lennon, 1940–1980)

1,432

Welcome to hell. Here's your accordion.

—Cartoon caption by Gary Larson

1,433

Accordions don't play "Lady of Spain," people do.

—Herb Caen (1916–1997)

1,434

I HAVE AN ACCORDION AND I'M NOT AFRAID TO USE IT.

—*Bumper sticker*

1,435

When you've heard one bagpipe tune, you've heard them both.

—*Jack Finney (1911–1995)*

1,436

Bagpipes are the missing link between music and noise.

—*E. K. Kruger*

1,437

Blood should be stirred before it's spilled, and nothing does it better than bagpipes.

—*Ervin Lewis*

1,438

Ignorance is no excuse for any crime except pop music.

—*Irma Kurtz*

1,439

The reason there are so many Jewish violinists is that our fingers are circumcised, which gives us very good dexterity.

—*Itzhak Perlman*

1,440

The oboe is an ill wind that nobody blows good.

—*Will Rogers (1879–1935)*

1,441

I played first chair in the high school band until they gave me an instrument.

—*George R. Hext*

1,442

When buying a used car, punch the buttons on the radio. If all the stations are rock and roll, there's a good chance the transmission is shot.

—*Larry Lujack*

1,443

The chief objection of playing a wind instrument is that it prolongs the life of the player.

—George Bernard Shaw (1856–1950)

1,444

I wish the government would put a tax on pianos for the incompetent.

—Dame Edith Sitwell (1887–1964)

1,445

My musical talent is less God-given than taketh away.

—Steve Rubenstein

1,446

Swans sing before they die; 'twer no bad thing
Should certain people die before they sing.

—*Samuel Taylor Coleridge (1772–1834)*

1,447

She was a soprano of the kind often used for augmenting grief at a funeral.

—*George Ade (1866–1944)*

1,448

I can hold a note as long as Chase National Bank.

—*Ethel Merman (1908–1984)*

1,449

Mozart was composing when he was six years old. When I was six, I was blowing into a shoehorn.

—John Kerwin

1,450

The hot music now is a combination of country and rap. It's called crap.

—Bud E. Luv

1,451

If you had it to do all over, George, would you fall in love with yourself again?

—Oscar Levant (1906–1972)
to George Gershwin (1898–1937)

1,452

The only winner in the war of 1812 was Tchaikovsky.

—Solomon Short

1,453

Men who listen to classical music tend not to spit.

—Rita Rudner

1,454

The cello has such a lugubrious sound, like someone reading a will.

—Irene Thomas (1919–2001)

1,455

Tonight's performance has been canceled because the star of the show has decided that musicals are stupid.

—Cartoonist Bruce Eric Kaplan

1,456

Nausea, Diarrhea, Projectile Vomiting, and Oily Discharge are the rock bands performing at the arena tonight.

—*Susie MacNelly*

1,457

I hate music, especially when it's played.

—*Jimmy Durante (1893–1980)*

1,458

After Rossini dies, who will be there to promote his music?

—*Richard Wagner (1813–1883)*

1,459

If I listen to too much Wagner, I get the urge to invade Poland.

—*Woody Allen*

1,460

I love Wagner, but the music I prefer is that of a cat hung up by its tail outside a window and trying to stick to the glass with its claws.

—*Charles Baudelaire (1821–1867)*

1,461

I don't care what language an opera is sung in so long as it is a language I don't understand.

—*Edward Appleton (1892–1965)*

1,462

No good opera plot can be sensible, for people do not sing when they are feeling sensible.

—*W. H. Auden (1907–1973)*

1,463

Only in opera do people die of love.

—*Freda Bright*

1,464

Going to an opera, like getting drunk, is a sin that carries its own punishment.

—*Hannah More (1745–1833)*

1,465

Beethoven sounds like the upsetting of a bag of nails with here and there a dropped hammer.

—*John Ruskin (1819–1900)*

1,466

If you combine what naturally attracts children—sex, violence, revenge, spectacle, and vigorous noise—what you have is grand opera.

—*Miss Manners (Judith Martin)*

1,467

I've had three wives and three guitars in my life, but I've flirted with others.

—*Andrés Segovia (1893–1987)*

ART

1,468

Michelangelo was a pornographer.

—*Camille Paglia*

1,469

Get this woman a Valium! Hand her a gin! Camille, honey, calm down!

—*Molly Ivins (1944–2007) on Camille Paglia*

1,470

Van Gogh became a painter because he had no ear for music.

—*Nikki Harris*

1,471

When I was a child, my mother said to me, "If you become a soldier, you'll be a general. If you become a monk, you'll end up as pope." Instead, I became a painter and ended up as Picasso.

—*Pablo Picasso (1881–1973)*

1,472

A portrait is a painting in which there is something wrong with the mouth.

—*Eugene Speicher (1883–1962)*

1,473

There are only two styles of portrait painting: the serious and the smirk.

—*Charles Dickens (1812–1870)*

1,474

Which painting would I save if there was a fire at the National Gallery? The one nearest the door.

—*George Bernard Shaw (1856–1950)*

1,475

Promises are like children's art—often made and seldom kept.

—*Peter Schickele*

1,476

All the good ideas I ever had came to me while I was milking a cow.

—Grant Wood (1891–1942)

1,477

See what will happen if you don't stop biting your fingernails?

—Will Rogers (1879–1935) to his niece while looking at the Venus de Milo

1,478

Mona Lisa looks as though she's about to be sick.

—Nöel Coward (1899–1973)

1,479

Leonardo da Vinci was going to paint Jesus feeding the multitudes, but lost interest and stopped at twelve, calling it the Last Supper.

—Tom Wisher

1,480

If you know Morse code, tap dancers drive you crazy.

—Mitch Hedberg (1968–2005)

1,481

We studied the Flemish masters using real phlegm.

—*Lew Cady*

1,482

Modern art is what happens when painters stop looking at girls and persuade themselves that they have a better idea.

—*John Ciardi (1916–1986)*

1,483

In comic strips, the character on the left always speaks first.

—*George Carlin (1937–2008)*

TELEVISION

1,484

The great thing about television is that if something important happens anywhere in the world, day or night, you can always change the channel.

—*From* Taxi

1,485

Television permits millions of people to hear the same joke at the same time and still remain lonesome.

—*T. S. Eliot (1888–1965)*

1,486

If you die horribly on television, you will not have died in vain. You will have entertained us.

—*Kurt Vonnegut (1922–2007)*

1,487

If it weren't for electricity, we'd all be watching television by candlelight.

—George Gobel (1919–1991)

1,488

The following program is rated *P* for Poop.

—Cartoonist Jack Ziegler

1,489

Dealing with network executives is like being nibbled to death by ducks.

—Eric Sevareid (1912–1992)

1,490

I won't eat any form of intelligent life, but I would gladly eat a network executive.

—Marty Feldman (1934–1982)

1,491

My father hated radio and couldn't wait for television to be invented so he could hate that, too.

—Peter De Vries (1910–1993)

1,492

Murder stories on television bring murder back into its rightful setting—the home.

—Alfred Hitchcock (1899–1980)

1,493

The trouble with television is that it takes your mind off your mind.

—Robert Orben

1,494

There are days when any electrical appliance in the house, including the vacuum cleaner, offers more entertainment than the TV set.

—Harriet Van Horne (1920–1998)

1,495

I try to be as ingratiating as possible without making myself vomit.

—Katie Couric

1,496

The best that can be said for Norwegian television is that it gives you the sensation of a coma without the worry.

—*Bill Bryson*

1,497

Men don't care what's on television. They only care about what else is on television.

—*Jerry Seinfeld*

1,498

Soap operas are slow-moving. If the *Titanic* had been one, it'd still be sinking.

—*Suzanne Somers*

1,499

Court TV has been named the official channel of the National Football League.

—*Jay Leno*

FASHION

1,500

Fashion is something that goes in one year and out the other.

—Unknown

1,501

Fashion can be bought, style one must possess.

—Edna Woolman Chase (1877–1957)

1,502

I keep fabric softener in my pockets so women won't cling to me.

—Larry Reeb

1,503

How many more bathroom-window curtains must die to clothe golfers?

—Mike Lough

1,504

I know this dress was a bargain because I overheard the clerk in the store say that I got it for a ridiculous figure.

—*Minnie Pearl (1912–1996)*

1,505

My Avon lady called and asked me not to tell where I got my cosmetics.

—*Margaret Hance (1923–1990)*

1,506

Have you ever taken something out of the clothes hamper because it was, relatively, the cleanest thing?

—Katharine Whitehorn

1,507

That's quite a dress you almost have on.

—Alan Jay Lerner in the film An American in Paris, *1951*

1,508

I got some new underwear today. Well, new to me.

—Emo Philips

1,509

The softer a man's head, the louder his socks.

—Helen Rowland (1876–1950)

1,510

You must either dress badly or spend more money than you wish to. Many women do both.

—Dame Rose Macaulay (1881–1958)

1,511

Women thrive on novelty and therefore are interested in fashion. Men prefer old pipes and torn jackets.

—*Anthony Burgess (1917–1993)*

1,512

I did not have 3,000 pairs of shoes. I had 1,060.

—*Imelda Marcos*

1,513

Anyone with more than 365 pairs of shoes is a pig.

—*Barbara Melser Lieberman*

1,514

If the shoe fits, it's ugly.

—*Gold's Law*

1,515

If the shoe fits, it's too expensive.

—*Adrienne Gusoff*

1,516

High heels were invented by a woman who had been kissed on the forehead.

—*Christopher Morley (1890–1957)*

1,517

Etiquette is for the guidance of those who have no manners, as fashion is for those who have no taste.

—*Queen Marie of Romania (1875–1938)*

1,518

In West Hollywood, cops shout, "Stop! Those shoes don't go with those pants!"

—*Robin Williams*

1,519

Englishwomen dress as if they had been a mouse in a previous incarnation or hope to be in the next.

—*Dame Edith Sitwell (1887–1964)*

1,520

Woman to man in a bar: "I thought I'd never laugh again. Then I saw your jacket."

—*Cartoon caption by Leo Cullum (1942–2010)*

1,521

She was a large woman who seemed not so much dressed as upholstered.

—J. M. Barrie (1860–1937)

1,522

What is Victoria's Secret? My guess is that she likes to dress as a slut.

—Carol Siskind

1,523

When you put clothes on, they tend to deteriorate with a strange rapidity and one feels so sorry for them.

—Joyce Grenfell (1910–1979)

1,524

The important thing about lipstick is to accept God's word on where your lips end.

—Jerry Seinfeld

1,525

If I had been born a man, I would have become a transvestite.

—Dolly Parton

1,526

I don't know how long it takes to do my hair because I'm never there when they do my hair.

—Dolly Parton

1,527

John Madden is a man who didn't let success go to his clothes.

—Mike Ditka

1,528

He was a tubby little chap who looked like he had been poured into his clothes and had forgotten to say, "When."

—P. G. Wodehouse (1881–1975)

1,529

Friendship is not possible between two women if only one of them is well dressed.

—Laurie Colvin

1,530

Never wear a hat that has more character than you do.

—Michael Harris

1,531

If you wear a dinner jacket, don't wear anything else on it, like lunch or dinner.

—*George Burns (1896–1996)*

1,532

If women dressed for men, stores wouldn't have much to sell except an occasional sun visor.

—*Groucho Marx (1890–1977)*

1,533

The sense of being well dressed gives a feeling of inward tranquillity that religion is powerless to bestow.

—*Miss C. F. Forbes (1817–1911)*

1,534

I wish I could grow a mustache. It's like having a little pet on your face.

—*Anita Wise*

1,535

I decided long ago not to look at the right side of menus or the price tag on clothes—otherwise I would have starved, naked.

—*Helen Hayes (1900–1993)*

1,536

Clothes don't make the man, God does. Stop taking credit, my pants.

—*Stephen Colbert*

1,537

If you are pear-shaped, don't wear pear-colored clothes.

—*Demetri Martin*

1,538

My luggage was sent to Israel by mistake, where it was opened and my clothes altered.

—*Woody Allen*

1,539

If you are all wrapped up in yourself, you are over-dressed.

—*Kate Halvorson*

1,540

From a fashion point of view, the pope is only one hat away from being the grand wizard of the Ku Klux Klan.

—Jon Stewart

1,541

My wife and I can put tattoos on our buttocks without fear of negative publicity.

—One of Stanley Bing's sixteen reasons why he's glad he isn't famous

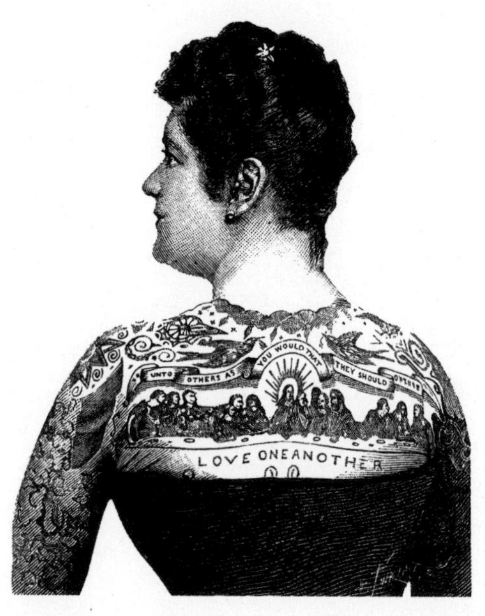

1,542

Wear sweatpants to bed so that when you get up, you're already dressed.

—Cynthia Heimel

1,543

Don't think of shopping for clothes as shopping. Think of it as hunting.

—Jane Hall

1,544

I'm a blonde that prefers gentlemen.

—Barbara Eden

1,545

He is every other inch a gentleman.

—Barbara Eden

ANIMALS

1,546

Of all the noxious animals, the most noxious is the tourist.

—Francis Kilvert (1840–1879)

1,547

Never call anyone a baboon unless you are sure of your facts.

—Will Cuppy (1884–1949)

1,548

The eagle may soar, but the weasel never gets sucked into a jet engine.

—John Benfield

1,549

Never buy a pit bull from a one-armed man.

—Unknown

1,550

Britain plans to ban the breeding of pit bulls. It's hard enough to put a muzzle on a pit bull; lots of luck with those condoms.

—Jay Leno

1,551

If a pit bull romances your leg, fake an orgasm.

—Hut Landon

1,552

Don't let sleeping dogs lie. Insist on the truth.

—Cynthia Nelms

1,553

My dog is worried about the economy because Alpo is up to $1.66 a can. That's almost $12 in dog money.

—Joe Weinstein

1,554

Dogs are wolves without ideals.

—Unknown

1,555

Other dogs look at French poodles and wonder if they are members of a weird religious sect.

—Rita Rudner

1,556

Dogs never bite me. Just humans.

—Marilyn Monroe (1926–1962)

1,557

It is fair to say that I am a friend to the creatures of the earth when I'm not busy eating them or wearing them.

—John Hodgman

1,558

Insects are the general rule and everything else is a special case.

—Paul Bystrak (1921–2010)

1,559

In my former life I was a sanitary landfill.

—Garfield *(Jim Davis)*

1,560

Cats are a waste of fur.

—Rita Rudner

1,561

Every life should have nine cats.

—Unknown

1,562

If cats could talk, they would lie.

—J. Kopack

1,563

I don't know why cats are such habitual vomiters. A dog is going to bark. A cat is going to vomit.

—Roy Blount, Jr.

1,564

If dogs could talk, they'd say things like "Hey! Hey! Hey! Hey!"

—Ellen DeGeneres

1,565

Confront a child, a puppy, and a kitten with a sudden danger; the child will turn instinctively for assistance, the puppy will grovel in abject submission, and the kitten will brace its tiny body for resistance.

—Saki (H. H. Munro, 1870–1916)

1,566

I can't decide between a dog and a child. Should I ruin my rug or my life?

—Rita Rudner

1,567

If your dog is fat, you aren't getting enough exercise.

—Unknown

1,568

The noblest dog is the hot dog, which feeds the hand that bites it.

—Laurence J. Peter (1919–1990)

1,569

If there are no dogs in heaven, then when I die, I want to go where they went.

—Unknown

1,570

All dogs don't go to heaven; only those who've accepted Christ.

—Stephen Colbert

1,571

I sleep with five cats. The trouble is, they react the same to a moth as an ax murderer. Either I get a hole in the head or in my sweater.

—Paula Poundstone

1,572

A friend of mine left $15,000 to her cat. Today that cat is broke.

—Ann Landers (1918–2002)

1,573

The cat left the room.

—Snoopy, on being told by Lucy to write something that would please everybody (Charles Schulz, 1922–2000)

1,574

We have a cat named Ben Hur. We called it Ben until it had kittens.

—Sally Poplin

1,575

Nature abhors a vacuum, but not as much as a cat does.

—*Nelson A. Crawford*

1,576

If you hold a cat by the tail, you learn things you cannot learn any other way.

—*Mark Twain (1835–1910)*

1,577

Every woman should have four pets in her life—a mink in her closet, a jaguar in her garage, a tiger in her bed, and a jackass who pays for everything.

—*Paris Hilton*

1,578

The best pet is the cow. Cows will love you and never ask anything in return. They will be your friend forever. And when you tire of them, you can kill them and eat them.

—*Bill Bryson*

1,579

My favorite animal is steak.

—*Fran Lebowitz*

1,580

People who live in glass houses must like dead birds.

—*Robert Brenneman*

1,581

You can lead a herring to water, but you have to walk really fast or it will die.

—*From* The Golden Girls

1,582

I had a parrot that didn't know how to say, "I'm hungry," so it died.

—*Mitch Hedberg (1968–2005)*

1,583

Every year, back comes spring with nasty little birds yapping their fool heads off and the ground all mucked up with plants.

—*Dorothy Parker (1893–1967)*

1,584

I used to get up at dawn, partly because I was ambitious and partly because my neighbor bought a rooster.

—*Tom Wisher*

1,585

Horse sense is what keeps horses from betting on people.

—W. C. Fields (1880–1946)

1,586

I put my money on a great horse. It took seven horses to beat him.

—Henry "Henny" Youngman (1906–1998)

1,587

A horse is dangerous at both ends and uncomfortable in the middle.

—Ian Fleming (1908–1964)

1,588

If the horse is dead, dismount.

—Terry Paulson

1,589

The lovebird is 100 percent faithful to its mate, as long as they are locked together in the same cage.

—Will Cuppy (1884–1949)

1,590

What separates us from all other animals is that we aren't afraid of vacuum cleaners.

—Jeff Stilson

1,591

Mickey is more than a mouse to me. I am honored to call him a friend.

—Annette Funicello

1,592

If it weren't for gravity, birds would just stay up in the air until they died.

—Steven Wright

1,593

Some of my best leading men have been dogs and horses.

—Elizabeth Taylor (1932–2011)

1,594

All animals look like somebody.

—Cynthia Nelms

1,595

I crossed a crow with a cuckoo. I got a raven maniac.

—*Jay Johnson*

1,596

Cross a termite with a praying mantis and you get a bug that says grace before eating your house.

—*Unknown*

1,597

Somebody open the door! The flies haven't been out all day!

—*Redd Foxx (1922–1991) on* Sanford and Son

1,598

My dog is not a child substitute, according to its pediatrician.

—*Rita Rudner*

1,599

Mice and bears live in harmony in nature. They can't mate, though, or the mouse would explode.

—*From* The Golden Girls

1,600

My dog doesn't bite, but he is sometimes sarcastic.

—Charlie Brown (Charles Schulz, 1922–2000)

1,601

I spilled Spot remover on my dog and now he's gone.

—Steven Wright

1,602

Never tell your dog he's adopted.

—Unknown

1,603

A Chihuahua looks like a dog far away.

—Billiam Coronell

1,604

Outside of a dog, a book is probably a man's best friend. Inside a dog it's too dark to read.

—Groucho Marx (1890–1977)

1,605

Humans have all the qualities of dogs except loyalty.

—W. C. Fields (1880–1946)

1,606

Dogs' lives are too short. Their only fault, really.

—Carlotta Monterey O'Neill (1888–1970)

1,607

Barking dogs never bite—at least not while they're barking.

—Louis A. Safian

1,608

Scientists tell us that the fastest animal on earth, with a top speed of 120 feet per second, is a cow dropped from a helicopter.

—Dave Barry

1,609

Some people lose all respect for the lion unless he devours them instantly. There is no pleasing some people.

—Will Cuppy (1884–1949)

1,610

I am fond of pigs. Dogs look up to us. Cats look down on us. Pigs treat us as equals.

—*Winston Churchill (1874–1965)*

1,611

Infant warthogs resemble both sides of the family.

—*Will Cuppy (1884–1949)*

1,612

My husband bought a staple gun. Now we have to bring food to the cat.

—*Rita Rudner*

1,613

As every cat owner knows, nobody owns a cat.

—*Ellen Perry Berkeley*

1,614

I'd horsewhip you if I had a horse.

—*S. J. Perelman (1904–1979)*

1,615

If you are being chased by a shark, you don't have to swim faster than the shark, only faster than the person you're with.

—*Kevin Nealon*

1,616

All modern men are descended from wormlike creatures, but it shows more on some people.

—*Will Cuppy (1884–1949)*

1,617

The microbe is so very small
You cannot take him out at all.

—*Hilaire Belloc (1870–1953)*

1,618

The cow is of the bovine ilk;
One end is moo, the other milk.

—*Ogden Nash (1902–1971)*

1,619

When insects take over the world, I hope they remember how we used to take them along on picnics.

—*Bill Vaughan (1915–1977)*

1,620

Do racehorses know they are racing? I think all they know is that the jockey is in a hurry.

—*Jerry Seinfeld*

TRAVEL

1,621

Never trust anything you read in a travel article.

—Dave Barry

1,622

I have paid as much as $300 a night to throw up in a sink shaped like a seashell.

—Erma Bombeck (1927–1996)

1,623

When I travel, I'm always late and the orgy has moved elsewhere.

—Mordecai Richler (1931–2001)

1,624

A hotel minibar allows you to see into the future and what a Pepsi will cost in 2020.

—Rich Hall

1,625

Agoraphobia—don't leave home without it.

—*Ben "Rivethead" Hamper*

1,626

Is this a pleasure trip or is your husband with you?

—*Bill Hoest,* The Lockhorns *(1926–1988)*

1,627

The only aspect of our travels that is interesting to others is disaster.

—*Martha Gellman*

1,628

Americans have always liked travel, that being how we got here in the first place.

—*Otto Friedrich (1929–1995)*

1,629

People travel to faraway places to watch in fascination the kind of people they ignore at home.

—*Dagobert Runes (1902–1982)*

1,630

After Orville Wright's historic twelve-second flight in 1903, his luggage could not be found.

—*Cartoon caption by S. Harris*

1,631

We must be the worst family in town. Maybe we should move to a larger one.

—*Bart Simpson (Matt Groening)*

1,632

Never travel without food in your pocket—if only to throw at attacking dogs.

—*E. S. Bates*

1,633

Dorothy got lost in Oz because three men were giving her directions.

—*Unknown*

1,634

When a man meets catastrophe on the road, he looks in his wallet, while a woman looks in the mirror.

—*Margaret Turnbull (1872–1942)*

1,635

The reason it takes a million sperm to find an egg is that none of them will stop to ask for directions.

—Adam Ferrara

1,636

At what age is it appropriate to tell a highway it's adopted?

—Zach Galifianakis

1,637

Most of life consists of driving somewhere and then returning home wondering why you went.

—John Updike (1932–2009)

1,638

Once you see the drivers in Indonesia, you understand why religion plays such a big part in their lives.

—Erma Bombeck (1927–1996)

1,639

Europe is so rich in history that sometimes you can barely stand it.

—Dave Barry

1,640

The worse thing about Europe is that you can't go out in the middle of the night and get a Slurpee.

—*Former pro basketball player Tellis Frank*

1,641

The great and recurring question about abroad is, is it worth getting there?

—*Dame Rose Macaulay (1881–1958)*

1,642

Instead of learning a foreign language, I grow hair under my arms.

—*Sue Kolinsky*

1,643

Traveling is the ruin of all happiness. There is no looking at a building once you've seen Italy.

—*Fanny Burney (1752–1840)*

1,644

It's easier to find a traveling companion than to get rid of one.

—*Art Buchwald (1925–2007)*

1,645

Attention! The train arriving at platforms eight, nine, ten, and eleven is arriving sideways.

—Unknown

1,646

The airlines have come up with a new fee. From now on, a scrotum will be classed as a carry-on bag.

—Stephen Colbert

1,647

Fly first class or your kids will.

—Unknown

1,648

If God wanted us to fly, he would have given us tickets.

—Mel Brooks

1,649

When are the airlines going to offer half fares to Pago, Bora, Baden, and Walla?

—Bob Holmes

1,650

Next time you fly, squirt ketchup on each ear and then ask the flight attendant, "Is this supposed to happen?"

—Brad Stine

1,651

I feel about airplanes the same way I feel about diets, that they are wonderful things for other people to go on.

—Jean Kerr (1922–2003)

1,652

According to a new law, all airline food must taste like something.

—David Letterman

1,653

Flight attendant: "In case of a drop in cabin pressure, an oxygen mask will drop down in front of you for two dollars."

—Cartoon caption by Robert Leighton

1,654

I stayed in a hotel that promised to treat me as well as my own mother. When I checked out, the clerk said, "Go ahead and leave, I'll be dead in a few weeks anyway."

—*Rita Rudner*

1,655

If it is tourist season, can we shoot them?

—*Nick Featherman*

1,656

If you reject the food, ignore the customs, fear the religion, and avoid the people, you might as well stay home.

—*James Michener (1907–1997)*

1,657

I'm not the type who wants to go back to the land. I'm the type who wants to go back to the hotel.

—*Fran Lebowitz*

1,658

The difference between wandering and traveling is that we wander for distraction and we travel for fulfillment.

—*Hilaire Belloc (1870–1953)*

1,659

Camping is nature's way of promoting the motel business.

—*Dave Barry*

1,660

If 70 percent of the earth's surface is covered by water, how come it's so hard to get to the beach?

—*Teressa Skelton*

1,661

When at sea, avoid the land.

—*Nautical saying*

1,662

The only reason they say, “Women and children first,” is to test the strength of the lifeboats.

—*Judy Allen*

1,663

Coming off the freeway, I saw a guy with a sign that said, “If you were homeless, you’d be home now.”

—*John Mendoza*

1,664

IF YOU CAN READ THIS, I’VE LOST MY TRAILER.

—*Bumper sticker*

1,665

HORN DOESN’T WORK. WATCH FOR FINGER.

—*Bumper sticker*

1,666

BACK OFF OR I'LL FLUSH.

—*Bumper sticker on a mobile home*

1,667

If you have attention deficit disorder, can you drive a Ford Focus?

—*Zach Galifianakis*

1,668

If you're lost in the woods, play solitaire with a pack of cards. Someone is sure to show up and tell you to play the red jack on the black queen.

—*Unknown*

1,669

If I had asked people what they wanted, they would have said faster horses.

—*Henry Ford (1863–1947)*

1,670

I learned to drive on my dad's lap. He'd work the brakes, I'd work the wheel. When I took the driver's test,

I sat on the examiner's lap. I failed the test, but he still writes to me.

—Garry Shandling

1,671

My wife and I fly free because of her job. She's a terrorist.

—Brian Kiley

1,672

A hotel is a place that keeps the makers of twenty-five-watt lightbulbs in business.

—Shelley Berman

1,673

Rome is like a man who keeps himself by showing visitors the corpse of his grandmother.

—James Joyce (1882–1941)

1,674

What a pity, when Christopher Columbus discovered America, that he ever mentioned it.

—Margot Asquith (1864–1945)

1,675

The thing that impressed me most about America is the way parents obey their children.

—Edward, the Duke of Windsor (1894–1972)

1,676

Washington, DC, is to lying what Wisconsin is to cheese.

—Dennis Miller

1,677

The trouble with New York is that it's so convenient to everything I can't afford.

—Jack Barry (1918–1984)

1,678

I moved to New York City for my health. I'm paranoid and it was the only place where my fears were justified.

—Anita Weiss

1,679

New York City is the only city in the world where you can be awakened by a smell.

—Jeff Garlin

1,680

In New York City, one suicide in ten is attributed to a lack of storage space.

—*Judith Stone*

1,681

If you're not in New York, you're camping out.

—*Thomas Dewey (1902–1971)*

1,682

I prefer New York to Los Angeles because I get paid three hours earlier.

—*Henry "Henny" Youngman (1906–1998)*

1,683

Hell is New York City with all the escape hatches sealed.

—*James R. Frakes*

1,684

If you get New Yorkers out of the city for two weeks to detox, they are like everybody else.

—*Pat Schroeder*

1,685

ENTERING NEW YORK CITY—NOW WITH FEWER HOMICIDES.

—Billboard suggested by Michael Maslin

1,686

Being miserable and treating everybody like dirt is every New Yorker's God-given right.

—From the movie Ghostbusters II, *1989*

1,687

New York is the city that never sleeps, which is why it looks like hell in the morning.

—Bill Maher

1,688

If a day goes by in New York and I haven't been slain, I'm happy.

—Carol Leifer

1,689

There is so little greenery in New York City it would make a stone sick.

—Nikita Khrushchev (1894–1971)

1,690

The two best things about traveling are arriving in a new city and leaving it.

—*Unknown*

1,691

The heaviest baggage for a traveler is an empty purse.

—*English saying*

1,692

New York is the most exciting place in the world to live. There are so many ways to die here.

—*Denis Leary*

1,693

I'm an octoroon. When I walk down the street in New York, I get harassed by everyone. It makes me feel pretty.

—*Mo Rocca*

1,694

In other parts of the country, couples try to stay together for the sake of the children. In New York, they try to work things out for the sake of the apartment.

—*David Sedaris*

1,695

When it's three o'clock in New York, it's still 1938 in London.

—*Bette Midler*

1,696

In New York, everyone is an exile, none more so than the Americans.

—*Charlotte Perkins Gilman (1860–1935)*

1,697

The Bronx?
No thonx!

—*Ogden Nash (1902–1971)*

1,698

When I applied for a library card, the clerk said I had to prove I was a resident of New York City, so I stabbed him.

—*Emo Philips*

1,699

In Miami, there are rallies for the right to sacrifice chickens.

—*Dave Barry*

1,700

Edith was a little country bounded on the north, south, east, and west by Edith.

—*Martha Ostenso (1900–1963)*

1,701

In Greenville, South Carolina, I saw a guy autographing books he had read.

—*Jack Simmons*

1,702

In California schools, Chief Crazy Horse is called either Chief Sitting Dude or Chief Mentally Impaired Horse because the word *crazy* might offend those who are crazy.

—*Joe Queenan*

1,703

The main attraction in Beverly Hills is the Tomb of the Unknown Servant.

—Steve Bluestein

1,704

If Los Angeles is not the rectum of civilization, then I am not an anatomist.

—H. L. Mencken (1880–1956)

1,705

Moving from Los Angeles to Petaluma is the best thing I ever did. I like having neighbors who aren't writing screenplays.

—Rick Reynolds

1,706

Great God! This is an awful place!

—Captain Robert Falcon Scott (1868–1912)
on reaching the South Pole

1,707

The trouble with Spokane is that there's nothing to do there after ten in the morning.

—Jim Murray (1919–1998)

1,708

Hell is a city much like London.

—Percy Bysshe Shelley (1792–1822)

1,709

Branson, Missouri, is Las Vegas for the toothless.

—Dennis Miller

1,710

Not everybody in the Ozarks lives in a house trailer. There's a huge waiting list.

—Nancy Newton

1,711

The prefrontal region of the Peking Man resembles that found in some parts of the Middle West.

—Will Cuppy (1884–1949)

1,712

The Midwest is a place where people got through the 1980s without ever tasting balsamic vinegar.

—Rebecca Christian

1,713

While flying over Milwaukee, the pilot announced that watches should be set back one hundred years.

—*Jack E. Leonard (1910–1973)*

1,714

South Dakota would only lose about six months if somebody bombed it back to the Stone Age.

—*Gregg Rogell*

1,715

I was born in Alabama, but I left after one month because I had already done all there was to do.

—*Paula Poundstone*

1,716

In the beginning, Atlanta was a void without form. It still is.

—*Roy Blount, Jr.*

1,717

The average Southerner has the speech patterns of somebody slipping in and out of consciousness.

—*Bill Bryson*

1,718

Jesus said that the meek would inherit the earth. So far, all we've got is Minnesota and North Dakota.

—Garrison Keillor

1,719

The meek shall inherit the earth. They won't have the nerve to refuse it.

—Jackie Vernon (1924–1987)

1,720

Eat, drink, and be merry, for tomorrow you may be in Utah.

—Unknown

1,721

You should climb Mount Fuji once in your life. Climb it twice and you're a fool.

—Japanese saying

1,722

Suburbia is a place where developers cut down the trees and name streets after them.

—Bill Vaughan (1915–1977)

1,723

Home is where you hang your head.

—*Unknown*

1,724

He who laughs last is probably British.

—*Unknown*

1,725

Geography! It's where it's at.

—*Unknown*

1,726

WELCOME TO KANSAS OR SOME STATE VERY MUCH LIKE IT.

—*Highway sign in a Robert Mankoff* New Yorker *cartoon*

1,727

If you grew up in Minnesota, you'll never be warm again.

—*Garrison Keillor*

1,728

During blizzards in Minnesota, there is an increase in cannibalism.

—*Garrison Keillor*

1,729

Sometimes it's so cold in Minnesota you have to wear two condoms.

—*Bruce Lansky*

1,730

In Arizona, a baby's first words are "But it's a dry heat."

—*Wil Shiner*

1,731

I'm a city boy. When I hunt, it's for a parking place, when I fish, it's for compliments.

—*Jon Carroll*

1,732

A neighborhood is a residential area that is changing for the worse.

—*John Ciardi (1916–1986)*

1,733

France is the only country in the world where you can make love in the afternoon without somebody banging on the door.

—*Barbara Cartland (1901–2000)*

1,734

Those French! They have a different word for everything!

—*Steve Martin*

1,735

Canada was built on dead beavers.

—*Margaret Atwood*

1,736

A Canadian is merely an unarmed American with good health care.

—*John Wing*

1,737

The Lord said, "Let there be wheat," and Saskatchewan was born.

—*Stephen Leacock (1869–1944)*

1,738

Canada is not the party. Canada is the apartment above the party.

—*Craig Ferguson*

1,739

No leaders ever get overthrown in Canada because nobody gives a damn.

—Mordecai Richler (1931–2001)

1,740

I have no opinion on New Zealand because when I was there, it seemed to be closed.

—Clement Freud (1924–2009)

1,741

Speaking of irony, there's a newspaper in Britain called the *Sun*.

—Stewart Francis

1,742

Why was I born Scandinavian? The food is bad, the weather is terrible, and the theology can break a man's heart.

—Garrison Keillor

1,743

America is an adorable woman chewing tobacco.

—Frédéric-Auguste Bartholdi (1834–1904),
designer of the Statue of Liberty

1,744

I come from a small town where the population never changes. Every time a woman gets pregnant, someone leaves town.

—Michael Pritchard

1,745

I've seen the Leaning Tower of Pisa. It's a tower and it's leaning. You look at it, but nothing happens. So then you look for some place to get a sandwich.

—Danny DeVito

SPORTS

1,746

Sports are the toy department of life.

—*Howard Cosell (1918–1995)*

1,747

Fishing is boring until you catch a fish, when it becomes disgusting.

—*Dave Barry*

1,748

Teach a man to fish and he eats for a day. Teach him how to fish and you get rid of him for the whole weekend.

—*Zenna Schaffer*

1,749

I fish, therefore I lie.

—*Tom Clark*

1,750

The first time I walked into a trophy shop, I looked around and thought to myself, "This guy is *good*!"

—*Fred Wolf*

1,751

You miss 100 percent of the shots you don't take.

—*Wayne Gretzky*

1,752

I quit coaching because of illness and fatigue. The fans were sick and tired of me.

—*John Ralston*

1,753

There are two kinds of coaches, those who have been fired and those who will be fired.

—*Ken Loeffler*

1,754

A horseshoe can't bring good luck because every horse in the race carries four.

—*Walter "Red" Smith (1905–1982)*

1,755

Saint Bernard is the patron saint of skiers who need brandy.

—*Rich Hall*

1,756

Humility is something I've always prided myself on.

—*NFL quarterback Bernie Kosar*

1,757

I know it's going to be a bad night when I see elderly women playing Frisbee with flattened road squirrels.

—*Johnny Carson (1925–2005)*

1,758

Anybody who watches three games of football in a row should be declared brain-dead.

—*Erma Bombeck (1927–1996)*

1,759

Football combines the two worst things about American life: violence punctuated by committee meetings.

—*George Will*

1,760

Nobody in football should be called a genius. A genius is somebody like Norman Einstein.

—*Former quarterback Joe Theismann*

1,761

Women don't box because they don't want to weigh in.

—*Unknown*

1,762

The quarterback's wife is pregnant. It's nice to know he finally hit his intended receiver.

—*Unknown*

1,763

Open your parachute when cars look as big as ants. If ants look as big as cars, you've waited too long.

—*Ernst Luposchainsky*

1,764

Just because nobody complains doesn't mean all parachutes are perfect.

—*Benny Hill (1925–1992)*

1,765

Do you have any problems other than that you're unemployed, a moron, and a dork?

—*John McEnroe to a fan*

1,766

Winners aren't popular; losers often are.

—*Virginia Wade*

1,767

When I coached at Niagara, we gave recruits a piece of caramel candy. If they took the wrapper off before eating it, they got a basketball scholarship; otherwise they got a football scholarship.

—*Frank Layden*

1,768

Australians are good at sports because of a total absence of any kind of intellectual distraction.

—*Dame Edna Everage (Barry Humphries)*

1,769

Chess is as elaborate a waste of human intelligence as you can find outside an advertising agency.

—*Raymond Chandler (1888–1959)*

1,770

My computer beats me at chess, but it is no match for me in kickboxing.

—*Emo Philips*

1,771

Checkers is safer to play than chess because in checkers you can't fall asleep and get a king stuck in your eye.

—*Jim Loy*

1,772

Children are the best opponents in Scrabble because they are easy to beat and fun to cheat.

—*Fran Lebowitz*

1,773

Never read by candlelight anything smaller than the ace of clubs.

—*Sir Henry Halford (Henry Vaughn, 1766–1844)*

1,774

Many people play a fair game of golf . . . if you watch them.

—*Joey Adams (1911–1999)*

1,775

I don't watch golf on television because I can't stand people who whisper.

—David Brenner

1,776

Golf is one of the few sports where a white man can dress like a black pimp.

—Robin Williams

1,777

Give me golf clubs, fresh air, and a beautiful partner and you can keep the clubs and the fresh air.

—Jack Benny (1894–1974)

1,778

Golf is the only sport where the object is to play as little as possible.

—Charles G. McLoughlin

1,779

Golf was originally restricted to the wealthy, but today is open to anybody with hideous clothing.

—*Dave Barry*

1,780

Nothing increases your golf score like witnesses.

—*Unknown*

1,781

When I play golf, I spend so much time in the woods that my caddy has to check me for ticks.

—*Jeff Foxworthy*

1,782

I regard golf as an expensive way of playing marbles.

—*G. K. Chesterton (1874–1936)*

1,783

I took me seventeen years to get three thousand hits in baseball. I did it one afternoon playing golf.

—*Hank Aaron*

1,784

Golf and sex are the only things you can enjoy without being good at them.

—*Jimmy Demaret (1910–1983)*

1,785

Golf is a puzzle without an answer.

—*Gary Player*

1,786

A personal tragedy leads to six stages of grief: shock, denial, pain, anger, depression, and acceptance. It's the same after a round of golf.

—Unknown

1,787

I play in the low eighties. If it's hotter than that, I won't play.

—Joe E. Lewis (1902–1971)

1,788

If you're going to throw a club, throw it ahead of you down the fairway so you don't have to waste energy going back to pick it up.

—Tommy Bolt (1916–2008)

1,789

Putting allows the touchy golfer two to four chances to blow a gasket.

—Tommy Bolt (1916–2008)

1,790

You can make a lot of money playing golf. Just ask my ex-wives.

—Lee Trevino

1,791

I deny the allegations made by Bob Hope that during my last round of golf I hit an eagle, a birdie, an elk, and a moose.

—President Gerald Ford (1913–2006)

1,792

The first time I played the Masters I was so nervous I drank a bottle of rum before teeing off. I shot the happiest 83 of my life.

—Chi Chi Rodriguez

1,793

I don't fear death, but I do three-footers for par.

—Chi Chi Rodriguez

1,794

If you think it's hard to meet new people, try picking up the wrong golf ball.

—Jack Lemmon (1925–2001)

1,795

If I had to choose between my wife and my putter, I'd miss her.

—*Gary Player*

1,796

Golf appeals to the idiot in us and the child. Just how childlike golfers become is shown by their frequent inability to count past five.

—*John Updike (1932–2009)*

1,797

If profanity had an influence on the course of balls, many games would be played much better than they are.

—*Unknown*

1,798

Inside every jogger is a potato yearning for a couch.

—*Robert Fredericks*

1,799

Croquet is a very good game for people who are annoyed with each other as it gives many opportunities for venting rancor.

—*Dame Rose Macaulay (1881–1958)*

1,800

It may well be that all games are silly, but then so are human beings.

—Robert Lynd (1879–1949)

1,801

Some days you're a windshield, some days you're a bug.

—Price Cobb, after winning a car race in 1988

1,802

When I left high school, they retired my jersey, but it was for sanitary reasons.

—George Carlin (1937–2008)

1,803

My philosophy was, like, people basically suck.

—Mike Tyson

1,804

I was wondering why the baseball was getting bigger—then it hit me.

—Unknown

1,805

A family of Cuban refugees landed in Florida. The first thing they did was take a bus to Chicago and beat the Cubs 6–3.

—*David Letterman*

1,806

Hating the New York Yankees is as American as apple pie, unwed mothers, and cheating on your income tax.

—*Mike Royko (1932–1997)*

1,807

God is good and will prove it when He takes even Mets fans into heaven.

—*Fritz Peterson*

1,808

Although he is a very poor fielder, he is a very poor hitter.

—*Ring Lardner (1885–1933)*

1,809

The secret of managing a baseball team is to keep the guys who hate you away from the ones who are undecided.

—*Casey Stengel (1890–1975)*

1,810

I knew when my career was over. In 1965 my baseball card came out with no picture.

—*Bob Uecker*

1,811

Sporting goods companies pay me not to endorse their products.

—*Bob Uecker*

1,812

When I came up to bat with three men on and two outs in the ninth, I'd look over to the other team's dugout and the players would already be in street clothes.

—*Bob Uecker*

1,813

You are a foul ball in the line drive of life.

—*Lucy to Charlie Brown (Charles Schulz, 1922–2000)*

1,814

Every time a baseball player grabs his crotch it makes him spit. That's why you should never date a baseball player.

—*Marsha Warfield*

1,815

A man once told me to walk with the Lord. I'd rather walk with the bases loaded.

—Ken Singleton

1,816

If he raced his pregnant wife, he'd finish third.

—Baseball coach Tommy Lasorda on a slow player

1,817

Trying to sneak a fastball past Hank Aaron was like trying to sneak a sunrise past a rooster.

—Joe Adcock (1927–1999)

1,818

Don't chew gum at the plate. It makes your eyeballs bounce up and down.

—Harmon Killebrew (1936–2011)

1,819

If at first you don't succeed, try for second.

—Unknown

1,820

If at first you don't succeed, deny trying.

—*Unknown*

1,821

If at first you don't succeed, try pitching.

—*Jack Harshman*

1,822

If at first you don't succeed, forget skydiving.

—Unknown

1,823

If you get three strikes, not even the best lawyer in the world can get you off.

—Bill Veeck (1914–1986)

1,824

If a tie is like kissing your sister, losing is like kissing your grandmother with her teeth out.

—George Brett

1,825

Trying is the first step toward failure.

—Homer Simpson (Matt Groening)

1,826

I forgot to say something during yesterday's game and it bears repeating.

—Sportscaster Ron Fairly

1,827

Slips of the tongue and mind made by snooker commentators on British television:

The match has gradually and suddenly come to a climax.

Well, velour was the better part of discretion there.

The audience is literally electrified and glued to their seats.

The audience is standing to relieve themselves.

I'm monosyllabic, if that's the word.

When Higgins has his tail up, he's a hard nut to crack.

I'm speechless! That says it all.

As for you, I don't know about me, I'm ready for bed.

—*From* Snooker Scene *magazine*

1,828

I met a woman in a bar who wore so much makeup that the pool players used her face to chalk their cues.

—*Larry Reeb*

1,829

The game of billiards has destroyed my naturally sweet disposition.

—*Mark Twain (1835–1910)*

1,830

I've been playing pool since Moby-Dick was a guppy.

—Rudolf Wanderone (Minnesota Fats, 1913–1996)

1,831

I went to Hong Kong to play pool with Happy the Chinaman and he ain't smiled since.

—Rudolf Wanderone (Minnesota Fats, 1913–1996)

1,832

Blacks don't skydive or bungee jump. It's exciting and dangerous enough just being black.

—From the movie The Original Kings of Comedy, *2000*

1,833

Sports are dangerous and tiring activities performed by people with whom I have nothing in common except the right to trial by jury.

—Fran Lebowitz

1,834

Earthquakes are helpful if you're bowling.

—Henry Cho

1,835

There are never any lines at the bathroom at a public swimming pool.

—*Dan Bradley*

1,836

Dogsled riding is both relaxing and fragrant.

—*Dave Barry*

1,837

It makes no difference if you lose until you lose.

—*Unknown*

1,838

When it comes to basketball, the NCAA owes a lot to the NAACP.

—*Cynthia Louise Laffoon*

1,839

If cocaine were helium, the NBA would float away.

—*Art Rust, Jr. (1927–2010)*

1,840

If you can't be an athlete, be an athletic supporter.

—*From the movie* Grease, *1978*

1,841

The difference between being in a relationship and prison is that in prison they let you play softball on weekends.

—*Bobby Kelton*

1,842

A recent study shows that 75 percent of the body's heat escapes through the head. That means you could ski naked if you had a good hat.

—*Jerry Seinfeld*

1,843

The breakfast of champions is not cereal, it's the opposition.

—*Nick Seitz*

CRIME

1,844

To reduce the chances of crime in your home, put a dead bolt in your door, put a peephole in your door, and move your door to Fresno, California.

—*Malcolm Kushner*

1,845

There are two kinds of criminals, those who get caught and the rest of us.

—*Unknown*

1,846

Few men have enough virtue to withstand the highest bidder.

—*George Washington (1732–1799)*

1,847

A criminal is a person with predatory instincts who lacks the capital to form a corporation.

—Howard Scott

1,848

I've killed so many houseplants that my photo is on WANTED posters in nurseries.

—Rita Rudner

1,849

We live in an age where pizza gets to your home before the police.

—Jeff Marder

1,850

Police records show that no woman has ever shot her husband while he was doing the dishes.

—Earl Wilson (1907–1987)

1,851

The reason there is so little crime in Germany is that it's against the law.

—Alex Levin

1,852

Sure, postal workers occasionally go on shooting sprees, but who doesn't?

—*Joel Stein*

1,853

I still miss my ex-husband, but my aim is improving.

—*Roseanne Barr*

1,854

In South Africa, the police dogs are part hyena. After they bite you, they laugh.

—*Pieter-Dirk Uys*

1,855

You are more likely to get shot by a fat cop if you run.

—*Dennis Miller*

1,856

Where I grew up, you could walk ten blocks and never leave the scene of a crime.

—*Charlie Callas (1927–2011)*

1,857

Aside from the killings, Washington, DC, has one of the lowest crime rates in the country.

—*Mayor Marion Barry*

1,858

The worst part about prison is the snoring.

—*Dr. Jack Kervorkian (1928–2011)*

1,859

I'd wish you luck, but for all I know you're planning to kill me.

—*Jackie Mason*

1,860

When you call 911 in New York City, the operator says, "This better be good."

—*David Letterman*

1,861

A man who has never gone to school can steal from a freight car, but if he has a university education, he can steal the whole railroad.

—*Franklin Delano Roosevelt (1882–1945)*

1,862

Don't worry about people stealing your ideas. Even if your ideas are good, you'll have to ram them down people's throats.

—Howard Aiken (1900–1973)

1,863

For a thief, stealth makes wealth.

—Leo Roberts

1,864

My father invented the burglar alarm—and then somebody stole it from him.

—Victor Borge (1909–2000)

1,865

There's no satisfaction in hanging a man who does not object to it.

—George Bernard Shaw (1856–1950)

1,866

Not all Sicilians are in the Mafia. Some of us are in the witness protection program.

—Tammy Pescatelli

1,867

More university graduates become criminals every year than policemen.

—*Philip Goodheart*

1,868

The rain it raineth on the just
And on the unjust fella;
But chiefly it raineth on the just
Because the unjust steals the just's umbrella.

—*Unknown*

1,869

One prisoner to another: "I said, 'Doc, it hurts when I go like this.' He said, 'Don't go like that.' So I killed him. What are you in for?"

—*Cartoonist Evan Forsch*

1,870

In parts of America today, it's more acceptable to carry a handgun than a pack of cigarettes.

—*Katharine Whitehorn*

1,871

The world would be better off as a nudist colony. No concealed weapons!

—*Cyra McFadden*

1,872

I think our police are excellent, probably because I haven't done anything that has occasioned being beaten up by them.

—*Sir Clement Freud (1924–2009)*

1,873

Australia started out as a prison colony while America is evolving into one.

—*Argus Hamilton*

1,874

A concrete truck has collided with a prison van. Motorists should watch for hardened criminals.

—*Ronnie Corbett*

1,875

I have never served on a jury because I am usually the accused.

—*Robert Pinske*

1,876

A jury consists of twelve people chosen to decide who has the better lawyer.

—Robert Frost (1874–1963)

1,877

This trial is a travesty; it's a travesty of a mockery of a sham of a mockery of a sham of a mockery of a travesty of two mockeries of a sham. I move for a mistrial.

—Woody Allen in Bananas, *1971*

1,878

A window of opportunity for me usually involves a rock.

—Jay London

1,879

Your Honor, I can't plead guilty or not guilty because I haven't yet heard the evidence.

—Jonathan S. Benton

1,880

Honesty is the best policy, but insanity is a better defense.

—Steve Landesberg (1936–2010)

1,881

Honesty is the best policy if nothing can be gained by lying.

—*Leo Roberts*

1,882

If you ever see me getting beat up by the police, put down your video camera and help me.

—*Robert "Bobcat" Goldthwait*

WORKING

1,883

All paid jobs degrade the mind.

—Aristotle (384–322 BC)

1,884

There is something wrong with my eyesight. I can't see going to work.

—Teddy Bergeron

1,885

A lot of people quit looking for work as soon as they get a job.

—Zig Ziglar

1,886

I have a set of motivational tapes, but I never feel like watching them.

—Daniel Liebert

1,887

Never argue with a man whose job depends on not being convinced.

—H. L. Mencken (1880–1956)

1,888

If women can sleep their way to the top, how come they aren't there?

—Ellen Goodman

1,889

There is always room at the top . . . after the investigation.

—Oliver Herford (1863–1935)

1,890

The glass ceiling melts when you turn up the heat.

—Pauline Kezer

1,891

If you are irreplaceable you will never be promoted.

—Jonathan S. Benton

1,892

Consultants have credibility because they are not dumb enough to work at any company.

—Dilbert *(Scott Adams)*

1,893

Engineers like to solve problems. If there aren't any, they will create some.

—Dilbert *(Scott Adams)*

1,894

Sometimes the choice is kick ass or kiss ass.

—*James Caan*

1,895

You learn more from getting your butt kicked than from getting it kissed.

—*Tom Hanks*

1,896

Success is the ability to rise above principle.

—*Gerald Barzan*

1,897

When my boss asked me if I could adopt a more positive attitude, I said, "I don't see why not."

—Jay Trachman (1939–2009)

1,898

I had a boring office job. I cleaned the windows in the envelopes.

—Rita Rudner

1,899

To get something done, give it to the busiest man you know and he'll have his secretary do it.

—Unknown

1,900

A desk is a dangerous place from which to watch the world.

—John Le Carré

1,901

Opportunities are usually disguised as hard work, so most people don't recognize them.

—Ann Landers (1918–2002)

1,902

You won't hear opportunity knock if the TV is on.

—*Unknown*

1,903

Opportunity knocked. My doorman threw him out.

—*Adrienne Gusoff*

1,904

Behind every failure is an opportunity somebody wishes they had missed.

—*Lily Tomlin*

1,905

A real job is a job you hate.

—*Bill Watterson*

1,906

If FedEx merged with UPS, the employees would be called FedUps.

—*Julia Byrne*

1,907

Never hire a career counselor. The best job they could get was career counselor.

—Dilbert *(Scott Adams)*

1,908

What I don't like about office Christmas parties is looking for a job afterwards.

—Phyllis Diller

1,909

I became a magician when my sister told me she got $100 a trick.

—Michael Finney

1,910

I saw two signs at a gas station: SELF-SERVICE and HELP WANTED. So I went in and hired myself.

—Steven Wright

1,911

The best jobs are coroner and mortician. The worst that can happen is that you find a pulse.

—Dennis Miller

1,912

The ability to sleep with your eyes open is an essential skill for those in middle or upper management.

—Ralph Noble

1,913

I think, therefore I'm overqualified.

—Unknown

1,914

If your ship doesn't come in, swim out to it.

—Jonathan Winters

1,915

I once got a job as a stripper. I took off my jewelry and said, "According to Jewish law, I'm now naked."

—*Charisse Savarin*

1,916

My worst job was selling phones over the phone. I'd call people, and if they answered, I'd hang up because they already had one.

—*Reno Goodale*

1,917

You're not fired, Harris. I'm just having you frozen until things pick up again.

—*Cartoon caption by Ed Arno (1916–2008)*

1,918

America has the most productive workers in the world. You know the little tags on so many products that say MADE IN CHINA? We make those.

—*Steve Bridges as Barack Obama*

1,919

Never hire an electrician whose eyebrows are scorched.

—*Mason Wilder*

1,920

Having men work alongside women is like having grizzly bears work alongside salmon.

—*Patrice O'Neal*

1,921

In the world of big corporations, there's nothing more lucrative than to be fired well.

—*Calvin Trillin*

1,922

Power is the ability not to have to please.

—*Elizabeth Janeway (1913–2005)*

1,923

There is nothing so useless as doing something efficiently that shouldn't be done at all.

—*Peter Drucker (1909–2005)*

1,924

Freedom is not caring about the quality of your work.

—Dilbert *(Scott Adams)*

1,925

They laughed when I said I wanted to be a comedian. Well, they're not laughing now.

—*Steve Altman*

1,926

Corollaries of Murphy's Law:

Everything takes longer than it takes.

Mrs. Murphy's Law: it's Mr. Murphy's fault.

Muprhy's Law: spelling errors will be noticed too late to correct.

Anything worth doing has already been done; therefore, nothing is worth doing.

Osborn's Law: variables won't, constants aren't.

Cole's Law: shredded cabbage.

—*From the Internet*

1,927

There is glory in a great mistake.

—*Nathalia Crane (1913–1998)*

1,928

Consultants usually have gray hair and hemorrhoids. The gray hair makes them look distinguished and the hemorrhoids make them look concerned.

—*Maxine, the Crabby Lady (John Wagner)*

1,929

A stressful job is one where you have to work with other people.

—*Maxine, the Crabby Lady (John Wagner)*

1,930

I was hired for a job in an information booth with no questions asked.

—*Jay London*

1,931

My retirement plan is a slippery floor in a department store.

—*Keith McGill*

1,932

After what happened to my 401(k), my retirement plan now is the Rapture.

—*Scott Dunn*

1,933

A woman's work is never done by a man.

—*Susan Richman*

1,934

Hard work never killed anybody who supervised it.

—*Harry C. Bauer*

LAWYERS

1,935

Lawyers should be buried at sea because deep down they're all right.

—*Unknown*

1,936

A lawyer with a briefcase can steal more than a thousand men with guns.

—*Mario Puzo (1920–1999)*

1,937

A town that can't support one lawyer can always support two.

—*Unknown*

1,938

There is no shortage of lawyers in Washington, DC. In fact, there may be more lawyers than people.

—*Sandra Day O'Connor*

1,939

I do not care to speak ill of a man behind his back, but I believe he is an attorney.

—*Samuel Johnson (1709–1784)*

1,940

We plead not guilty, Your Honor, and thanks for asking.

—*Cartoon caption by Frank Cotham*

1,941

I broke a mirror and now face seven years of bad luck. My lawyer thinks he can get me five.

—*Steven Wright*

1,942

Only lawyers and mental defectives are exempt from jury duty.

—*George Bernard Shaw (1856–1950)*

1,943

In the halls of justice, the only justice is in the halls.

—*Lenny Bruce (1925–1966)*

1,944

The law, in its majestic equality, forbids the rich as well as the poor to sleep under bridges, to beg in the streets, and to steal bread.

—*Anatole France (1844–1924)*

1,945

Justice is my being allowed to do whatever I want. Injustice is whatever prevents me from doing it.

—*Samuel Butler (1835–1902)*

1,946

Truth doesn't ring true in a court of law.

—*Enid Bagnold (1889–1981)*

1,947

If it were not for lawyers, we wouldn't need them.

—*A. K. Griffin*

BOREDOM

1,948

Somebody's boring me. I think it's me.

—*Dylan Thomas (1914–1953)*

1,949

A bore is a person who talks when you want him to listen.

—*Ambrose Bierce (1842–1914)*

1,950

A bore is a person not interested in you.

—*Mary Pettibone Poole (dates unknown)*

1,951

The secret of being a bore is to tell everything.

—*Voltaire (1694–1778)*

1,952

When you're bored with yourself, marry and be bored with someone else.

—*David Pryce-Jones*

1,953

There is something curiously boring about somebody else's happiness.

—*Aldous Huxley (1894–1963)*

1,954

I am one of those unhappy persons who inspire bores to the greatest flights of art.

—*Dame Edith Sitwell (1887–1984)*

1,955

No one really listens to anyone else, and if you try it for a while, you'll see why.

—*Mignon McLaughlin (1913–1983)*

1,956

Bored to death . . . it's as good a way to go as any other.

—*Peter Ustinov (1921–2004)*

1,957

Bores bore each other, too, but it never seems to teach them anything.

—*Don Marquis (1878–1937)*

1,958

A healthy adult bore consumes each year one and a half times his own weight in other people's patience.

—*John Updike (1932–2009)*

1,959

A gossip is one who talks to you about others, a bore talks to you about himself, and a brilliant conversationalist talks to you about you.

—*Lisa Kirk (1925–1990)*

1,960

Some people stay longer in an hour than others can in a week.

—*William Dean Howells (1837–1920)*

1,961

American men are obsessed with money, American women with weight. The men talk of gain, the women talk of loss, and I don't know which talk is the more boring.

—*Marya Mannes (1904–1990)*

MONEY

1,962

Noah was smart. At the lumberyard before building the ark, knowing that everybody there would be lost in the flood, he took out a loan payable in forty days and forty nights.

—*Tom Wisher*

1,963

The easiest way for your children to learn about money is for you not to have any.

—*Katharine Whitehorn*

1,964

Givers have to set limits because takers rarely do.

—*Irma Kurtz*

1,965

An unhappy poor person is in a better position than an unhappy rich person because he has hope. He thinks money will help.

—Jean Kerr (1922–2003)

1,966

The road to Easy Street goes through the sewer.

—John Madden

1,967

The greater the wealth, the thicker the dirt.

—John Kenneth Galbraith (1908–2006)

1,968

Don't talk about money with people who have much more or much less than you do.

—Katharine Whitehorn

1,969

If babies scream when they're hungry, what sound will they make later when they're audited?

—Rita Rudner

1,970

The nation should have a tax system that looks like someone designed it on purpose.

—*William E. Simon (1927–2000)*

1,971

The tax code is ten times bigger than the Bible without the good news.

—*Dave Camp, 2011 chairman of the Ways and Means Committee*

1,972

Death is the most convenient time to tax the rich.

—*David Lloyd George (1863–1945)*

1,973

At tax time, gather those receipts, get out the tax forms, sharpen your pencil, and stab yourself in the aorta.

—*Dave Barry*

1,974

Next to being shot at and missed, nothing is quite as satisfying as an income tax refund.

—*F. J. Raymond*

1,975

Be wary of strong drink. It can make you shoot at a tax collector and miss.

—*Robert Heinlein (1907–1988)*

1,976

Everybody likes a kidder, but nobody lends him money.

—*Arthur Miller (1915–2005)*

1,977

My problem is reconciling my gross habits with my net income.

—*Errol Flynn (1909–1959)*

1,978

My children didn't have my advantages. I was born into abject poverty.

—*Kirk Douglas*

1,979

It's a good thing that men make more money than women because otherwise they'd marry each other.

—*Mike Birbiglia*

1,980

People in a fortunate position always attribute it to virtue.

—John Kenneth Galbraith (1908–2006)

1,981

Don't pay a dollar for a bookmark. Just use the dollar.

—Fred Stoller

1,982

Riches don't make a man richer, only busier.

—From the movie 1492: Conquest of Paradise, *1992*

1,983

Having money is just the best thing.

—Madonna

1,984

Lack of money is the root of all evil.

—George Bernard Shaw (1856–1950)

1,985

Girls just wanna have funds.

—Adrienne Gusoff

1,986

A penny urned is a penny saved.

—Jerome Mannheim

1,987

A penny for your thoughts, if I'm not being too extravagant.

—Bill Hoest, The Lockhorns *(1926–1988)*

1,988

Those who have money have in their pockets those who have none.

—Leo Tolstoy (1828–1910)

1,989

If you want to know what God thinks of money, look at the people he gives it to.

—Maurice Baring (1874–1945)

1,990

Put your money in weeds. The price of weeds never goes down.

—*Wanda Sykes*

1,991

I opened an E-Trade account and in only a week I changed $1,000 into $420. Of course, I had to pay some fees.

—*Mike Birbiglia*

1,992

On Wall Street, enough is never enough.

—Alison Leigh Cowan

1,993

Never confuse brains with a bull market.

—Unknown

1,994

Money is something you have to make in case you don't die.

—Max Asnas (1898–1968)

1,995

If I had my life to lead over again, I'd need more money.

—Jim Shock

1,996

I just need enough money to tide me over until I need more.

—Bill Hoest, The Lockhorns *(1926–1988)*

1,997

You have no idea how difficult it is to be the victim of benevolence.

—Jane Aiken Hodge (1917–2009)

1,998

My husband is so cheap he won't buy a newspaper. He walks along with the paperboy and asks him questions.

—Jim Bailey as Phyllis Diller

1,999

It isn't necessary to be rich and famous to be happy. It is only necessary to be rich.

—Alan Alda

2,000

If it weren't for professional sports, a lot of kids wouldn't even know what a millionaire looks like.

—Phyllis Diller

2,001

Gambling is getting nothing for something.

—Wilson Mizner (1876–1933)

2,002

I used to be a heavy gambler, now I just make mental bets. That's how I lost my mind.

—*Steve Allen (1921–2000)*

2,003

Any item you lose automatically doubles in value.

—*Mignon McLaughlin (1913–1983)*

2,004

I've got all the money I'll ever need, if I die by four o'clock.

—*Henry "Henny" Youngman (1906–1998)*

2,005

The avoidance of taxes is the only intellectual pursuit that carries any reward.

—*John Maynard Keynes (1883–1946)*

2,006

A fool and his honey are soon parted.

—*Charlie Caruso*

2,007

There was a time when a fool and his money were soon parted, but now it happens to everybody.

—*Adlai Stevenson (1900–1965)*

2,008

How did a fool and his money get together in the first place?

—*Nick Featherman*

2,009

Never rely on your friends for money or on your money for friends.

—*Dr. Mardy Grothe*

2,010

Money isn't everything, according to those who have it.

—*Malcolm Forbes (1919–1990)*

2,011

Save money. Someday it might be valuable again.

—*Unknown*

2,012

Bank of America has laid off thirteen thousand workers because the lines at the bank were too short.

—*Jay Leno*

2,013

Misers make wonderful ancestors.

—David Brenner

2,014

The trouble with borrowing money from China is that thirty minutes later you feel broke again.

—Steve Bridges as Barack Obama

2,015

Economic forecasters exist to make astrologers look good.

—Robert B. Reich

2,016

I have something no billionaire will ever have: enough.

—Joseph Heller (1923–1999)

2,017

I am proud to be paying taxes in the United States, but I would be just as proud for half the money.

—Arthur Godfrey (1903–1983)

SCIENCE AND TECHNOLOGY

2,018

Artificial intelligence is no match for natural stupidity.

—*Unknown*

2,019

For every action, there is an equal and opposite criticism.

—*Harrison's Postulate*

2,020

Nothing puzzles me more than time and space; and yet nothing puzzles me less because I never think of them.

—*Charles Lamb (1775–1834)*

2,021

Willie was a chemist;
Willie is no more
What Willie took for H_2O
Was H_2SO_4

—*One of many Little Willie poems*

2,022

I view the Internet not as an information highway but as an asylum filled with babbling loonies.

—*Mike Royko (1932–1997)*

2,023

Getting information off the Internet is like taking a drink from a fire hydrant.

—*Mitchell Kapor*

2,024

Mrs. Bill Gates doesn't like to hear her husband called Mr. Microsoft.

—*Unknown*

2,025

The phone company handles 84 billion calls a year—everything from kings, queens, and presidents to the scum of the earth.

—*Lily Tomlin as Ernestine the Operator*

2,026

The surest sign that intelligent life exists elsewhere in the universe is that it has never tried to contact us.

—Calvin and Hobbes *(Bill Watterson)*

2,027

The digital camera is great because it allows us to reminisce instantly.

—Demetri Martin

2,028

The day I made the remark about inventing the Internet, I was tired because I'd been up all night inventing the digital camera.

—Al Gore

2,029

Einstein's original theory of relativity is that time slows down when you are with relatives.

—Garrison Keillor

2,030

Einstein knows as much about psychology as I do about physics, so we had a very nice talk.

—Sigmund Freud (1856–1939)

2,031

Technological progress is like an ax in the hands of a pathological criminal.

—Albert Einstein (1879–1955)

2,032

The universe is made up of electrons, protons, neutrons, and morons.

—Andy Dappen

2,033

The four building blocks of the universe are fire, water, gravel, and vinyl.

—Dave Barry

2,034

The most important scientific tool is the eraser.

—Dr. Luna B. Leopold (1915–2006), US Geological Survey

2,035

The telephone is a good way to talk to people without having to offer them a drink.

—Fran Lebowitz

2,036

The formula "two and two make five" is not without its attractions.

—Fyodor Dostoyevsky (1821–1881)

2,037

Anyone told that the universe is expanding and contracting in pulsations of 80 million years has the right to ask, "What's in it for me?"

—*Peter De Vries (1910–1993)*

2,038

Flying is learning how to throw yourself at the ground and miss.

—*Douglas Adams (1952–2001)*

2,039

Gravity always wins.

—*Erma Bombeck (1927–1996)*

2,040

I would love to be a nerd, but I don't have what it takes.

—*David Diamond*

2,041

I'm giving up Google for Lent.

—*Cartoon caption by Victoria Roberts*

2,042

The world is round. It has no point.

—*Adrienne Gusoff*

2,043

In ancient times they had no statistics, so they had to fall back on lies.

—*Stephen Leacock (1869–1944)*

2,044

I'm a mad scientist at bottom. Give me an underground laboratory, half a dozen atom smashers, and a beautiful girl in a diaphanous veil waiting to be turned into a chimpanzee, and I care not who writes the nation's laws.

—*S. J. Perelman (1904–1979)*

2,045

If we are going to teach "creation science" as an alternative to evolution, then we should also teach the stork theory as an alternative to biological reproduction.

—*Judith Hayes*

2,046

I don't think I'm alone when I say that I'd like to see more and more planets fall under the ruthless domination of our solar system.

—*Jack Handey*

2,047

Life on earth is expensive, but at least we get a free trip around the sun every year.

—*Unknown*

2,048

There are too many cameras. I bought something the other day and the clerk told me it was also a camera. I said, "I just wanted a grapefruit."

—*Mike Birbiglia*

2,049

eBay was shut down for three hours, which led to a loss of $6 million worth of useless crap.

—*Colin Quinn*

2,050

An object in motion will continue in the wrong direction;
An object at rest will remain in the wrong place.

—*David Gerold*

2,051

When choosing between two competing theories, pick the one that doesn't involve a magic spell.

—*Emo Philips*

2,052

Those who meddle in the affairs of cats will find piss in their computers.

—*Bruce Graham*

2,053

Alaska senator Ted Stevens (1923–2010) explained that the Internet was "a series of tubes." When his computer was down, he thought his tubes were tied.

—*Chet Hurley*

2,054

Who is General Failure and why is he reading my hard disk?

—*Steven Wright*

2,055

In the computer world, hardware is anything you can hit with a hammer, software is what you can only curse at.

—*Unknown*

2,056

One thing computers can do that humans can't is sit in a sealed box for months.

—*Jack Handey*

2,057

Computers are like men because they have a lot of data but are still clueless. Computers are like women because once you acquire one you spend all your money on accessories.

—*Unknown*

2,058

Computers enable people to make more mistakes faster than any other invention with the possible exception of tequila.

—*Mitch Ratcliffe*

2,059

The inhumanity of the computer is that it is completely honest.

—Isaac Asimov (1920–1992)

2,060

Computers are like the Old Testament God, lots of rules and no mercy.

—Joseph Campbell (1904–1987)

2,061

Computers are everywhere. Now tattoo parlors have spell check.

—Jay Leno

2,062

We love our own cell phones but hate everyone else's.

—Joe Bob Briggs

TRUTH

2,063

Nobody speaks the truth when there is something they must have.

—Elizabeth Bowen (1899–1973)

2,064

Everybody lies, but it doesn't matter because nobody listens.

—Nick Diamos

2,065

They say the truth will set you free, but Uncle Edgar told the truth and the judge gave him six months.

—Redd Foxx (1922–1991) on Sanford and Son

2,066

The truth will set you free, but it will first piss you off.

—Gloria Steinem

2,067

Cynicism is an unpleasant way of saying the truth.

—*Lillian Hellman (1905–1984)*

2,068

I told my wife the truth: that I was seeing a psychiatrist. Then she told me the truth: that she was seeing a psychiatrist, two plumbers, and a bartender.

—*Rodney Dangerfield (1921–2004)*

2,069

There are some people so addicted to exaggeration that they can't tell the truth without lying.

—*Josh Billings (1818–1885)*

2,070

Keep your facts, I'm going with the truth.

—*Stephen Colbert*

2,071

There are times when lying is the most sacred of duties.

—*Eugène Labiche (1815–1888)*

2,072

Facts are like cows. If you look at them in the face hard enough, they generally go away.

—*Dorothy Sayers (1893–1957)*

2,073

Any fool can tell the truth, but it requires a man of some sense to lie well.

—*Samuel Butler (1835–1902)*

2,074

All truth goes through three stages. First, it is ridiculed. Second, it is violently opposed. Third, it is accepted as self-evident.

—*Arthur Schopenhauer (1788–1860)*

2,075

The advantage of telling the truth is that nobody ever believes it.

—*Dorothy Sayers (1893–1957)*

2,076

The color of truth is gray.

—*André Gide (1869–1951)*

HOOEY

2,077

Medium wanted for Halloween-night séance with bowling after. Must be psychic and carry a 130 average.

—*Unknown*

2,078

Maybe tomorrow's horoscope will run a correction and an apology.

—*Bill Watterson*

2,079

The human brain is a device to keep the ears from grating on one another.

—*Peter De Vries (1910–1993)*

2,080

The more crap you believe, the better off you are.

—*Charles Bukowski (1920–1994)*

2,081

I called the Psychic Hotline and was told that I was very gullible and would soon be poorer.

—*Unknown*

2,082

Depend on the rabbit's foot if you wish, but remember that it didn't work for the rabbit.

—*R. E. Shay*

2,083

I almost had a psychic girlfriend, but she left me before we met.

—*Steven Wright*

2,084

Advertisement: "Psychic Wanted—qualified person will know where to apply."

—*Jay Trachman (1939–2009)*

2,085

Never call a psychic who has caller ID.

—*Maxine, the Crabby Lady (John Wagner)*

2,086

Here's a headline you never see: "Psychic Wins Lottery."

—*Dennis Miller*

2,087

If only the aliens would keep the people they abduct.

—*Unnamed friend quoted by Carl Sagan (1934–1996)*

2,088

What's your sign? Mine's STOP.

—*Donna Gephart*

2,089

How many people here believe in telekinetic powers? Raise my hand.

—*Emo Philips*

2,090

Last night I played poker with tarot cards. I got a full house and four people died.

—*Steven Wright*

2,091

Nothing is as strong in human beings as the craving to believe in something that is obviously wrong.

—*Joel Aschenbach*

2,092

Every time somebody has acupuncture, a voodoo doll somewhere has a really bad day.

—*Caryn Leschen*

2,093

During Thanksgiving dinner, I broke a wishbone and made a wish. Everybody at the table got up and left! Those things really work!

—*Robert Orben*

2,094

You don't have to be a house to be haunted.

—*Emily Dickinson (1830–1886)*

2,095

The lowest number of UFO sightings is in North Dakota because people there are so depressed they never look up.

—*Chuck Bryant*

2,096

Homer Simpson to a group of aliens: "Don't eat me! I have a wife and children! Eat them."

—*From* The Simpsons *(Matt Groening)*

2,097

The margin of error in astrology is plus or minus 100 percent.

—*Calvin Trillin*

STUPIDITY

2,098

Smart people know when to play dumb.

—*Dr. Mardy Grothe*

2,099

Abraham Lincoln was born in a log cabin he built with his own hands.

—*Pennsylvania Representative Daniel Flood (1903–1994)*

2,100

There's nothing more dangerous than a resourceful idiot.

—Dilbert *(Scott Adams)*

2,101

To do my part for the environment, I've started a compost heap in the backseat of my car.

—*Janine Ditullio*

2,102

You might be a redneck if:

1. You think your family reunion is a good place to meet girls.
2. Your wife's hairdo was destroyed by a ceiling fan.

—*Jeff Foxworthy*

2,103

Never attribute to malice what can be adequately explained by stupidity.

—*Nick Diamos*

2,104

I always use my stepladder because I don't get along with my real ladder.

—*Harry Hill*

2,105

If you won't leave me alone, I'll find someone who will.

—*Unknown*

2,106

I may be a dumb blonde, but I'm not that blonde.

—*Patricia Neill*

2,107

My brain's not blond.

—Cybill Shepherd

2,108

I often put boiling water in the freezer, then whenever I want boiling water, I simply defrost it.

—Gracie Allen (1895–1964)

2,109

I have long known that it is part of God's plan for me to spend a little time with each of the stupidest people on earth.

—Bill Bryson

2,110

I tripped on an escalator and fell down the stairs for an hour and a half.

—Demetri Martin

2,111

I bought some powdered water but I didn't know what to add.

—Steven Wright

2,112

Behind every argument is someone's stupidity.

—Robert Benchley (1889–1945)

2,113

He tricked me into marrying him. He told me he was pregnant.

—Carol Leifer

2,114

Last night lying in bed looking at the stars, I realized that something had happened to the ceiling.

—Unknown

2,115

We only use 10 percent of our brains. Think what we could do if we used the other 60 percent.

—Ellen DeGeneres

2,116

Ninety percent of the people in the world are confirmed idiots. The rest are awaiting confirmation.

—Brian Hendrickson

2,117

Sometimes I think you have to take a stupid pill every morning to serve in the United States Senate.

—Arkansas Senator Dale Bumpers

2,118

If your eyes hurt after drinking coffee, try drinking it without the spoon in the cup.

—Norm Crosby

2,119

It is so pleasant to come across people more stupid than ourselves. We love them at once for being so.

—Jerome K. Jerome (1859–1927)

2,120

I examined my family tree and discovered that I was the sap.

—Rodney Dangerfield (1921–2004)

2,121

Life is hard, but it's harder if you're stupid.

—Redd Foxx (1922–1991)

2,122

I've been up and down so many times I feel as if I'm in a revolving door.

—Cher

2,123

I watch a lot of baseball on radio.

—Gerald Ford (1913–2006)

2,124

They laughed at Joan of Arc, but she went right ahead and built it anyway.

—Gracie Allen (1895–1964)

2,125

There is a fine line between bravery and stupidity.

—Tom Seaver

2,126

Never underestimate the power of human stupidity.

—Robert Heinlein (1907–1988)

POLITICS

2,127

Thank heavens we don't get all the government we pay for.

—*Will Rogers (1879–1935)*

2,128

For every action there is an equal and opposite government program.

—*Unknown*

2,129

The whole of the global economy is based on supplying the cravings of 2 percent of the world's population.

—*Bill Bryson*

2,130

The great nations of the world have always acted like gangsters and the small nations like prostitutes.

—*Stanley Kubrick (1928–1999)*

2,131

All men with power ought to be mistrusted.

—*James Madison (1751–1836)*

2,132

I have brains and a uterus and I use both.

—*Former Congresswoman Pat Schroeder*

2,133

In a democracy you vote first and take orders later. In a dictatorship you don't bother with voting.

—*Charles Bukowski (1920–1994)*

2,134

I could be through with the whole economic crap in five weeks . . . this is beginning to bore me.

—*Karl Marx (1818–1883) while writing* Das Kapital

2,135

The world would not be in such a snarl
If Marx had been Groucho instead of Karl.

—*Irving Berlin (1888–1989)*

2,136

If a politician found he had cannibals among his constituents, he would promise them missionaries for dinner.

—*H. L. Mencken (1880–1956)*

2,137

It has been said that at the end of the day, every politician is human. What about during the day?

—*Stephen Colbert*

2,138

A statesman is a successful politician who is dead.

—*Thomas Brackett Reed (1839–1902)*

2,139

A public servant is taught to work slowly but surly.

—*Eugene H. Bales*

2,140

There are too many men in politics and not enough elsewhere.

—*Hermione Gingold (1897–1987)*

2,141

My TV set shows C-SPAN and the Home Shopping Network at the same time. The other night I accidentally bought a congressman.

—*Bruce Baum*

2,142

Our forefathers should have fought for representation without taxation.

—*Fletcher Knebel (1911–1993)*

2,143

Liberty works better on paper than it does in practice.

—*Will Rogers (1879–1935)*

2,144

Every society honors its live conformists and its dead troublemakers.

—*Mignon McLaughlin (1913–1983)*

2,145

My country, right or wrong, is like saying my mother, drunk or sober.

—*G. K. Chesterton (1874–1936)*

2,146

It's useless to hold people to anything they say while they're in love, drunk, or running for office.

—*Shirley MacLaine*

2,147

A decision is what a man makes when he can't find anybody to serve on a committee.

—*Fletcher Knebel (1911–1993)*

2,148

If I am elected mayor of New York, the first thing I will do is demand a recount.

—*William F. Buckley, Jr. (1925–2008)*

2,149

There is no monument dedicated to the memory of a committee.

—*Lester J. Pourciau (1936–2009)*

2,150

Overexposure to committee meetings can lead to a staff infection.

—*Dr. Mardy Grothe*

2,151

If you see a snake, just kill it—don't appoint a committee on snakes.

—Ross Perot

2,152

If we had had more time for discussion, we probably would have made a great many more mistakes.

—Leon Trotsky (1879–1940)

2,153

Communism doesn't work because people like to own stuff.

—Frank Zappa (1940–1993)

2,154

The function of socialism is to raise suffering to a higher level.

—Norman Mailer (1923–2007)

2,155

Capitalism, communism . . . it's all garbage.

—Mstislav Rostropovich (1927–2007)

2,156

The intermediate stage between socialism and capitalism is alcoholism.

—Norman Brenner

2,157

I've been married to one Marxist and one fascist and neither would take out the garbage.

—Lee Grant

2,158

Our legislators put their heads together, thus forming a rock garden.

—Herb Caen (1916–1997)

2,159

Every nation ridicules other nations, and all are right.

—Arthur Schopenhauer (1788–1860)

2,160

I believe that all government is evil and that trying to improve it is largely a waste of time.

—H. L. Mencken (1880–1956)

2,161

Democracy is like a tambourine. Not everybody can be trusted with it.

—*John Oliver*

2,162

If God wanted us to vote, he would have given us candidates.

—*Jay Leno*

2,163

The best argument against democracy is a five-minute conversation with the average voter.

—*Winston Churchill (1874–1965)*

2,164

Once the people begin to reason, all is lost.

—*Voltaire (1694–1778)*

2,165

You can fool all of the people some of the time and some of the people all of the time, which is sufficient.

—*Rose King*

2,166

Government expands to absorb revenue and then some.

—*Tom Wicker (1926–2011)*

2,167

The supply of government exceeds the demand.

—*Lewis Lapham*

2,168

The government puts fluoride in our drinking water to make us complacent, but I don't care.

—*Pete Holmes*

2,169

Democracy is people of all races, creeds, and colors moving away from people of all races, creeds, and colors.

—*Johnny Carson (1925–2005)*

2,170

You've got to admit that each party is worse than the other.

—*Will Rogers (1879–1935)*

2,171

Suggested warning for the Ten Commandments: "Candidates for public office should not attempt more than six of these."

—*Hilaire Belloc (1870–1953)*

2,172

A statesman is a politician whose price is unknown.

—*Robert Brenneman*

2,173

Diplomacy: lying in state.

—*Oliver Herford (1863–1935)*

2,174

The word *politics* comes from *poly*, meaning "many," and *ticks*, meaning "bloodsucking parasites."

—*Larry Hardiman*

2,175

If you don't know how to lie, cheat, and steal, turn your attention to politics and learn.

—*Josh Billings (1818–1885)*

2,176

There is no credit to being a comedian when you have the whole government working for you. I don't even have to exaggerate.

—*Will Rogers (1879–1935)*

2,177

Citizens should go to Washington and take the administration out for an afternoon of electroshock.

—*Lewis Black*

2,178

I want to be buried in Chicago so I can stay active in politics.

—*Mark Russell*

2,179

If I wanted to go crazy, I would do it in Washington because it wouldn't be noticed.

—*Irwin S. Cobb (1876–1944)*

2,180

A diplomat can tell you to go to hell in a way that makes you look forward to the trip.

—*Caskie Stinnett (1911–1998)*

2,181

A patriot is a person who gets a parking ticket and rejoices because the system works.

—*Bill Vaughan (1915–1977)*

2,182

The governor of Texas is studying Spanish and will soon be bi-ignorant.

—*Molly Ivins (1944–2007)*

2,183

I hate being a bureaucrat and will resign as soon as I know the proper procedure.

—*Cartoon caption by Hector Breeze*

2,184

I always wanted to get into politics but was never light enough to make the team.

—*Art Buchwald (1925–2007)*

2,185

I hope the mass media won't twist my words by quoting me verbatim.

—*Tina Fey as Sarah Palin*

2,186

A cardinal rule of politics: never be caught in bed with a live man or a dead woman.

—*From the TV series* Dallas

2,187

People now take comedians seriously and politicians as a joke.

—*Will Rogers (1879–1935)*

2,188

A politician is a person who approaches every subject with an open mouth.

—*Adlai Stevenson (1900–1965)*

2,189

The trickle-down theory holds that if you feed the horse enough oats, some will pass through to the road for sparrows.

—*John Kenneth Galbraith (1908–2006)*

2,190

Years ago, fairy tales began with "Once upon a time . . ." Now it's "If I am elected . . ."

—*Carolyn Warner*

2,191

Prime ministers are wedded to the truth, but like other married couples they sometimes live apart.

—*Saki (H. H. Munroe, 1870–1916)*

2,192

The worst thing you can do to politicians is quote them verbatim.

—*Andy Logan*

2,193

For too long, men have been messing things up. It's time to give women an opportunity.

—*Senator Dianne Feinstein*

2,194

I'll never run for office because I'm afraid no woman will come forward and claim she had sex with me.

—*Garry Shandling*

2,195

It's easier to be a conservative than a liberal because it's easier to give the finger than a helping hand.

—*Mike Royko (1932–1997)*

2,196

It's a pity that politicians aren't bastards by birth instead of by vocation.

—*Katharine Whitehorn*

2,197

Politics is not a vocation, nor is it an avocation. It's an incurable disease.

—*Joseph T. Robinson (1872–1937)*

2,198

Dan Quayle said he was going to be a pit bull during the campaign. I'll bet that made all the fireplugs nervous.

—*Bill Clinton*

2,199

Politicians are the hardest to cure of all insane people.

—*Robert E. Lee (1807–1870)*

2,200

George Washington to his father: "But if I never tell a lie, how can I get to be president?"

—*Red Buttons (1919–2006)*

2,201

Calvin Coolidge slept more than any other president. He had no ideas, but he was not a nuisance.

—*H. L. Mencken (1880–1956)*

2,202

Calvin Coolidge looks as though he had been weaned on a pickle.

—*Alice Roosevelt Longworth (1884–1980)*

2,203

If you don't say anything, you won't be called upon to repeat it.

—*Calvin Coolidge (1872–1933)*

2,204

Warren G. Harding was a benign blank—a decent, harmless, laborious, hollow-headed mediocrity. [His English] reminded me of a string of wet sponges, of college yells, of dogs barking through endless nights. It was so bad a sort of grandeur crept into it.

—*H. L. Mencken (1880–1956)*

2,205

The people have spoken, the bastards.

—*Morris Udall (1922–1998) on losing an election*

2,206

The difference between a caucus and a cactus is that at a cactus the pricks are on the outside.

—*Morris Udall (1922–1998)*

2,207

Instead of giving politicians the keys to the city, it's better to change the locks.

—Doug Larson

2,208

Politicians who speak of health care don't seem to realize that it is their campaign speeches that make us sick.

—Bob Hope (1903–2003)

2,209

A fool and his money are soon elected.

—Will Rogers (1879–1935)

2,210

Politicians are like diapers. They should be changed frequently and for the same reason.

—Robin Williams

2,211

In order to be the master, the politician poses as the servant.

—Charles de Gaulle (1890–1970)

2,212

I must follow the people. Am I not their leader?

—*Benjamin Disraeli (1804–1881)*

2,213

If I return to earth in another life, I hope it's not during a Republican administration.

—*Timothy Leary (1920–1996)*

2,214

Republicans stand for raw, unbridled evil and greed and ignorance smothered in balloons and ribbons.

—*Frank Zappa (1940–1993)*

2,215

Keep things as they are—vote for the Sadomasochistic Party.

—*Unknown*

2,216

The reason there are two senators from each state is so that one can be the designated driver.

—*Jay Leno*

2,217

The politicians in Minnesota are so honest they must be retarded.

—*Mike Royko (1932–1997)*

2,218

In my home state of Louisiana, we bury the dead above-ground so we can get them to the polls quicker.

—*Lesley Stahl*

2,219

The great thing about democracy is that it gives every voter a chance to do something stupid.

—*Art Spander*

2,220

I shall be an autocrat, that's my trade; and the good Lord will forgive me, that's his.

—*Catherine the Great (1729–1796)*

2,221

Democracy in America proves that anyone can grow up to be president, and anyone who doesn't grow up can be vice president.

—*Johnny Carson (1925–2005)*

2,222

If we don't change direction soon, we'll end up where we're going.

—*Professor Irwin Corey*

2,223

Give me a one-handed economist. All my economists say, "On the other hand . . ."

—*Harry S. Truman (1884–1972)*

2,224

A bureaucrat is a Democrat who holds an office that a Republican wants.

—*Harry S. Truman (1884–1972)*

2,225

Richard Nixon inherited some good instincts from his Quaker forebears, but by diligent hard work he overcame them.

—James Reston (1909–1995)

2,226

Ronald Reagan: Most of His Polyps Were Benign.

—1984 campaign slogan suggested by Dave Barry

2,227

I am president of the most powerful nation on earth and I take orders from nobody except photographers.

—Harry Truman (1884–1972)

2,228

If the answer is "Jerry Brown," the question must be very strange.

—Patrick A. Lewis

2,229

When your opponent is drowning, throw him an anvil.

—James Carville

2,230

Most of our troubles stem from our inability to sit quietly in a room.

—*Blaise Pascal (1623–1662)*

2,231

I'm all for foreign aid, and the sooner we get it the better.

—*Bob Hope (1903–2003)*

2,232

A committee is a cul-de-sac down which ideas are lured and then quietly strangled.

—Barnett Cocks (1907–1989)

2,233

Leadership involves finding a parade and getting in front of it.

—John Naisbitt

2,234

Nationalism is the measles of mankind.

—Albert Einstein (1879–1955)

2,235

Alexander Hamilton started the US Treasury Department with nothing, and that's the closest our country has ever been to being even.

—Will Rogers (1879–1935)

2,236

When I ran for president, I had to win. It was the only way I could get Barack Hussein Obama off the no-fly list.

—Steve Bridges as Barack Obama

2,237

Contrary to reports, I did not take my 1988 election loss badly. I went home and slept like a baby . . . waking up every two hours and crying.

—Bob Dole

2,238

I may be young, but I'm the first president to reach Level 9 on Grand Theft Auto.

—Steve Bridges as Barack Obama

2,239

In the Soviet Union, everybody suspected everybody else of being a spy. You couldn't trust anybody. When I was born in the 1970s, my mother picked me up and shouted, "Who are you working for?"

—Kira Soltanovich

2,240

The right honorable gentleman's smile is like the silver fittings of a coffin.

—Benjamin Disraeli (1804–1881)
on a fellow member of parliament

2,241

Margaret Thatcher is:

Attila the Hen *(Clement Freud, 1924–2009)*

The Immaculate Misconception *(Norman St. John-Stevas)*

2,242

The House of Lords is a body of five hundred men chosen at random from the unemployed.

—*David Lloyd George (1863–1945)*

2,243

TO HELL WITH YOU. OFFENSIVE LETTER FOLLOWS.

—*Telegram received by Sir Alec Douglas-Home (1903–1995)*

2,244

The worst thing in the world, next to anarchy, is government.

—*Henry Ward Beecher (1813–1887)*

WAR

2,245

A visitor from Mars could easily pick out the civilized nations. They have the best implements of war.

—Herbert V. Prochnow (1897–1998)

2,246

War is a cowardly escape from the problems of peace.

—Thomas Mann (1875–1955)

2,247

War is a brain-spattering, windpipe-splitting art.

—Lord Byron (1788–1824)

2,248

If people were forced to eat what they kill, there would be no more war.

—Abbie Hoffman (1936–1989)

2,249

War is not nice.

—*Barbara Bush*

2,250

The Rules of War: The laws that make it illegal to hit below the toes.

—*Leo Rosten (1908–1997)*

2,251

Genghis Khan conquered Asia with an army only half the size of New York City's civil service.

—*Emmanuel Savas*

2,252

Peace on earth would be the end of civilization as we know it.

—*Joseph Heller (1923–1999)*

2,253

Fisher's First Law of Military Combat: if the enemy is within range, so are you.

—*Ross Fisher*

2,254

Why does the air force need new bombers? Have the people we're bombing been complaining?

—*Comedian George Wallace*

2,255

Vietnam was the first war fought without censorship. Without censorship, things can get terribly confused in the public mind.

—*General William Westmoreland (1914–2005)*

2,256

War, like German opera, is too long and too loud.

—*Evelyn Waugh (1903–1966)*

2,257

War doesn't determine who is right, only who is left.

—*Unknown*

2,258

War is just another government program.

—*Joseph Sobran (1946–2010)*

2,259

You can't shake hands with a clenched fist.

—*Indira Gandhi (1917–1984)*

2,260

How come the dove gets to be the symbol of peace? Why not the pillow? It has more feathers and doesn't have that dangerous beak.

—*Jack Handey*

2,261

When I was in the army, I lost my rifle and was charged $85. That's why in the navy the captain goes down with the ship.

—*Dick Gregory*

2,262

No plan survives contact with the enemy.

—*Field Marshal Helmuth Karl Bernhard von Moltke (1800–1891)*

2,263

War is a series of catastrophes that result in a victory.

—*Georges Clemenceau (1841–1929)*

2,264

The military budget expands, the education budget shrinks. No wonder we have smart bombs and dumb kids.

—*Jon Stewart*

2,265

No military personnel will be involved in the invasion. Instead, we will land shiploads of lawyers, wait a few days, then march into the capital amid the chaos of litigation.

—*Dan Piraro*

2,266

I would lead a revolution against the American government, but I just bought a hammock.

—*Zach Galifianakis*

2,267

Nobody shoulders a rifle in defense of a boardinghouse.

—*Bret Harte (1836–1902)*

2,268

An eye for an eye just leads to more blindness.

—*Margaret Atwood*

2,269

Iraq and Iran should be combined into one country called Irate.

—*Denis Leary*

2,270

During World War II, it was legal to kill a German, but kill one now and all hell breaks loose.

—*Fred Willard on* Fernwood 2-Night, *1977*

WRITING

2,271

Being a writer is like having homework every night for the rest of your life.

—*Lawrence Kasdan*

2,272

Writers will happen in the best of families.

—*Rita Mae Brown*

2,273

What we need are new clichés.

—*Samuel Goldwyn (1882–1974)*

2,274

A great many people now writing would be better employed keeping rabbits.

—*Dame Edith Sitwell (1887–1964)*

2,275

Ireland does for its writers and artists what the United States does for its oilmen—makes their gushings virtually tax free.

—*Wilfrid Sheed (1930–2011)*

2,276

It's amazing that the amount of news that happens every day always exactly fits the newspaper.

—*Jerry Seinfeld*

2,277

I never read the papers. There is far too much going on already without reading about it as well.

—*Alan Ayckbourn*

2,278

Rupert Murdoch exudes self-confidence like a Goth swaggering around Rome wearing an onyx toilet seat for a collar.

—*Clive James*

2,279

No self-respecting fish would be wrapped in a Murdoch newspaper.

—*Mike Royko (1932–1997)*

2,280

If some great catastrophe is not announced every morning in the newspaper, we feel a certain void.

—*Paul Valéry (1871–1945)*

2,281

Freedom of the press belongs to those who own the press.

—*Susan B. Anthony (1820–1906)*

2,282

If a young writer can refrain from writing, he shouldn't hesitate to do so.

—*André Gide (1869–1951)*

2,283

I would like to acknowledge my four writers, Matthew, Mark, Luke, and John.

—*Bishop Fulton J. Sheen (1895–1979)*

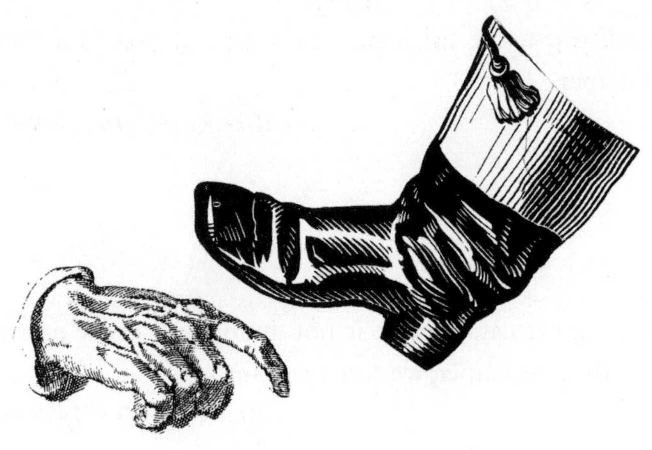

2,284

The moving finger writes. . . . Quick! Step on it!

—*Unknown*

2,285

Wanting to meet a writer because you like his work is like wanting to meet a duck because you like pâté.

—*Margaret Atwood*

2,286

Fiction is life with the dull bits left out.

—*Clive James*

2,287

Never use a big word when a little filthy one will do.

—*Johnny Carson (1925–2005)*

2,288

When one has no particular talent for anything, one takes to the pen.

—*Honoré de Balzac (1799–1850)*

2,289

Writing is like driving at night in the fog. You can only see as far ahead as your headlights, but you can make the whole trip that way.

—*E. L. Doctorow*

2,290

Writing is a socially acceptable form of schizophrenia.

—*E. L. Doctorow*

2,291

Letter from publisher to Snoopy: "We are sending you two rejection slips, one for your story and one for your next story."

—*Charles Schulz (1922–2000)*

2,292

This is the "between you and I" generation.

—*Eric Sevareid (1912–1992)*

2,293

Writing is like carrying a fetus.

—*Edna O'Brien*

2,294

Writing a book is like having a very long illness.

—*George Orwell (1903–1950)*

2,295

Critics? I love every bone in their heads.

—*Eugene O'Neill (1888–1953)*

2,296

The reason people become columnists is so they won't be interrupted.

—*Stefan Kanfer*

2,297

She plunged into a sea of platitudes and with powerful strokes of a Channel swimmer made her confident way toward the white cliffs of the obvious.

—*W. Somerset Maugham (1874–1965)*

2,298

You should always believe what you read in the newspapers because that makes them more interesting.

—*Dame Rose Macaulay (1881–1958)*

2,299

Writing only leads to more writing.

—*Colette (1873–1954)*

2,300

An author is a fool who, not content with boring those he lives with, insists on boring future generations.

—*Charles de Montesquieu (1689–1755)*

2,301

There is nothing to writing. All you do is sit at a typewriter and open a vein.

—*Walter "Red" Smith (1905–1982)*

2,302

Writing in a diary every day is like returning to one's own vomit.

—*Enoch Powell (1912–1998)*

2,303

I believe more in the scissors than the pencil.

—*Truman Capote (1924–1984)*

2,304

I am the literary equivalent of a Big Mac and fries.

—*Stephen King*

2,305

It's not who you know. It's whom.

—*Reverend Peter Gomes (1943–2011)*

2,306

For a lesbian bastard writer mental case, I'm doing awfully well.

—*Jill Johnston (1929–2010)*

2,307

Little Truman Capote had such a high-pitched voice that it could only be detected by bat.

—*Tennessee Williams (1911–1983)*

2,308

Truman Capote was a sweetly vicious old lady.

—*Tennessee Williams (1911–1983)*

2,309

William Faulkner said more asinine things than any other major American writer.

—*Norman Mailer (1923–2007)*

2,310

All you have to do to have an interesting life is to be a damned fool.

—*Saul Bellow (1915–2005)*

2,311

A figure of speech can often get into a crack too small for logic.

—*Unknown*

2,312

A journalist is a person who has missed his calling.

—*Otto von Bismarck (1815–1898)*

2,313

I could never understand when to use *lie* and when to use *lay*, which is why nobody goes to bed in my novels.

—*Willie Snow Ethridge (1900–1982)*

2,314

The way Shaw believes in himself is quite refreshing in these atheistic days when so many people believe in no God at all.

—*Israel Zangwill (1864–1926)*

2,315

When you were quite a little boy, somebody ought to have said, "Hush," just once.

—Mrs. Patrick Campbell (1865–1940) to George Bernard Shaw

2,316

Woman to author: "Your book nauseated me. Did you do that on purpose?"

—Cartoon caption by Robert Weber

2,317

His volumes speak silences.

—Cartoonist Bruce Eric Kaplan

2,318

If I didn't have writing, I'd be running down the street hurling grenades in people's faces.

—Paul Fussell

2,319

If Shakespeare had had to go on an author tour to promote *Romeo and Juliet*, he never would have written *Macbeth*.

—Dr. Joyce Brothers

2,320

I have tried to read Shakespeare and found it so intolerably dull that it nauseated me.

—Charles Darwin (1809–1882)

2,321

Bacon did not write Shakespeare. Shakespeare ate bacon.

—Professor Irwin Corey

2,322

I have suffered more ghastly evenings with Shakespeare than with any other dramatist.

—Peter Brock

2,323

It would positively be a relief to me to dig up Shakespeare and throw stones at him.

—George Bernard Shaw (1856–1950)

2,324

Let Shakespeare do it his way and I'll do it mine. We'll see who comes out ahead.

—Mae West (1893–1980)

2,325

Playing Shakespeare onstage is tiring. You never get to sit down unless you're the king.

—Josephine Hull (1883–1957)

2,326

Shakespeare was a dramatist of note
Who lived by writing things to quote.

—H. C. Bunner (1855–1896)

2,327

At times I think and at times I am.

—Paul Valéry (1871–1945)

2,328

I ink, therefore iamb.

—Adrienne Gusoff

2,329

Shakespeare murdered Hamlet, and many Hamlets have murdered Shakespeare.

—Evan Esar (1899–1995)

2,330

I know no person so perfectly disagreeable and even dangerous as an author.

—*William IV (1765–1837)*

2,331

A freelance writer is someone who is paid per piece, per word, or perhaps.

—*Robert Benchley (1889–1945)*

2,332

A writer is somebody for whom writing is more difficult than it is for other people.

—*Thomas Mann (1875–1955)*

2,333

Write what you know. That should leave you with a lot of free time.

—*Howard Nemerov (1920–1991)*

2,334

I would venture to guess that Anon, who wrote so much without taking credit, was a woman.

—*Virginia Woolf (1882–1941)*

2,335

We're still pretty far apart. I'm looking for a six-figure advance and they're refusing to read the manuscript.

—Cartoon caption by Robert Mankoff

2,336

Not reading poetry amounts to a national pastime in America.

—Phyllis McGinley (1905–1978)

2,337

I don't like to boast, but I have probably skipped more poetry than any other person of my age and weight in this country.

—Will Cuppy (1884–1949)

2,338

It is not widely known that you can sing most of the poems of Emily Dickinson to the tune of "The Yellow Rose of Texas."

—Garrison Keillor

2,339

A poet can write about a man slaying a dragon, but not about a man pushing a button and dropping a bomb.

—*W. H. Auden (1907–1973)*

2,340

I am returning the otherwise good typing paper to you because somebody has printed gibberish all over it and put your name on top.

—*Unknown editor*

2,341

If it sounds like writing, I rewrite it.

—*Elmore Leonard*

2,342

A writer's best friend is the incinerator.

—*Thornton Wilder (1897–1975)*

2,343

Poets are born, not paid.

—*Wilson Mizner (1876–1933)*

2,344

Poetry is what Milton saw when he went blind.

—Don Marquis (1878–1937)

2,345

Signs that your fetus will be a writer:

1. You have morning sickness at night because the fetus finds it too distracting to work during the day.
2. You develop cravings for typists.
3. Through a stethoscope you hear excuses.

—Fran Lebowitz in Metropolitan Life, *1978*

2,346

Media is the plural of mediocrity.

—Jimmy Breslin

2,347

The Society of Indexers should be known as Indexers, Society of, The.

—Keith Waterhouse (1929–2009)

BOOKS

2,348

I've been in love three hundred times in my life, and all but five were with books.

—Lee Glickstein

2,349

My personal hobbies are reading and silence.

—Dame Edith Sitwell (1887–1964)

2,350

Bookstore pickup line: Have you seen *Tax Tips for Billionaires*?

—David Letterman

2,351

The worst thing about new books is that they keep us from reading the old ones.

—Joseph Joubert (1754–1824)

2,352

An advantage of books is that they are easy to rewind. Close it and you're back at the beginning.

—*Jerry Seinfeld*

2,353

The oldest books are just out to those who haven't read them.

—*Samuel Butler (1835–1902)*

2,354

What a sense of superiority it gives one not to read a book that everybody else is reading.

—*Alice James (1848–1892)*

2,355

I wrote the story myself. It's about a girl who lost her reputation and never missed it.

—*Mae West (1893–1980)*

2,356

If you can explain how to write a book, then you don't know how to write one. If you can write a book, then you won't be able to explain how you did it.

—*Joe Bob Briggs*

2,357

The shelf life of the average trade book is somewhere between milk and yogurt.

—*Calvin Trillin*

2,358

Books should never be banned. The practice is as indefensible as infanticide.

—*Rebecca West (1892–1983)*

2,359

Every burned book illuminates the world.

—*Ralph Waldo Emerson (1803–1882)*

2,360

It was a book to kill time for those who like it better dead.

—Dame Rose Macaulay (1881–1958)

2,361

Books are a load of crap.

—Philip Larkin (1922–1985) in his poem "A Study of Reading Habits," 1964

2,362

A good heavy book holds you down. It's an anchor that keeps you from getting up and having another gin and tonic.

—Roy Blount, Jr.

2,363

Sign in bookstore window: BOOKS ON PAPER.

—Cartoon caption by Mike Twohy

2,364

I suppose all publishers are untrustworthy. They certainly always look it.

—Oscar Wilde (1854–1900)

2,365

Why are builders afraid to have a thirteenth floor but publishers aren't afraid of Chapter 11?

—*Unknown*

2,366

Publishers print nothing but sex novels now.

—*Guy Patin (1601–1672)*

2,367

I have only read one book in my life and that is *White Fang*. It was so frightfully good I never read another.

—*Nancy Mitford (1904–1973)*

2,368

I have known her to pass the whole evening without mentioning a single book, or in fact anything unpleasant at all.

—*Henry Reed (1914–1986)*

2,369

I asked the librarian where the self-help books were, and she said, "If I told you, it would defeat the whole purpose."

—*Brian Kiley*

2,370

The profession of book-writing makes horse racing seem like a solid, stable business.

—*John Steinbeck (1902–1968)*

2,371

I hesitate starting my autobiography too soon for fear of something important having not yet happened. Suppose I end my days as president of Mexico?

—Bertrand Russell (1872–1970) in a 1930 letter

2,372

Next to the writer of real estate ads, the autobiographer is the most suspect of prose artists.

—Donal Henahan

2,373

Great Moments in Literature, 1844: Mrs. Alexander Dumas says to her husband, "Why don't you make them the three musketeers instead of the three garbagemen?"

—Joe Martin

2,374

I think it's a cute idea, but the salespeople think there is no market for a big pop-up book of toxic waste.

—Cartoon caption by Robert Mankoff

2,375

Politically correct retitled books:

The Still-Productive Senior and the Sea (Steve Weisberger)

Crime and Time-Out (Gina Bryant)

Unresolved Labor/Management Dispute on the Bounty (Mark Severin)

—From The Week *magazine contest, January 28, 2011*

2,376

I wrote a children's book, but not on purpose.

—Steven Wright

2,377

When I get a little money, I buy books; if any is left over, I buy food and clothing.

—*Erasmus (1466–1536)*

2,378

Buying books would be a good thing if you could also buy the time to read them.

—*Arthur Schopenhauer (1788–1860)*

2,379

Condense soup, not books!

—*Jonathan S. Benton*

2,380

Most girls would rather lose an ovary
Than read *Madame Bovary*;
And boys prefer a banana enema
To reading *Anna Karenina*.

—*Leo Roberts*

PROVERBS

2,381

For every back there is a knife.

—*Corporate proverb*

2,382

The tears of strangers are only water.

—*Russian proverb*

2,383

Every bull has a bear behind.

—*Wall Street proverb*

2,384

If God lived on earth, people would break his windows.

—*Yiddish proverb*

2,385

"For example" is not proof.

—*Yiddish proverb*

2,386

The best things in life aren't things.

—*John Tigges (1932–2008)*

2,387

Many are called but few get up.

—*Oliver Herford (1863–1935)*

2,388

Build a man a fire and he will be warm for a day. Set a man on fire and he will be warm for the rest of his life.

—*Terry Pratchett*

2,389

When a rogue kisses you, count your teeth.

—*Hebrew proverb*

2,390

May the wind be always at your back, unless it's coming from you personally.

—*Irish proverb*

2,391

A word to the wise ain't necessary. It's the stupid who need the advice.

—*Bill Cosby*

2,392

Veni, vidi, vomiti. We came, we saw, we threw up.

—*Chet Hurley*

2,393

Never stand behind a sneezing cow.

—*Unknown*

2,394

A stopped clock is right twice a day, but a sundial can be used to stab someone, even at night.

—*John Hodgman*

ANSWERS

2,395

Excuse me, did you say something?
Answer to "Do you think I'm boring?"

—*Dick Cavalli*

2,396

A shot of bourbon.
Answer to "What's the best way for a writer to get started?"

—*Johnny Hart (1931–2007)*

2,397

Subordinate clauses.
Answer to "What do you call Santa's helpers?"

—*Don Wiles*

2,398

You mean now?
Answer to "What time is it?"

—Demetri Martin

2,399

Why, is one missing?
Answer to "Did you take a taxi?"

—Dean Martin and Jerry Lewis

2,400

In silence.
Answer to "How would you like your hair trimmed?"

—Archelaus (23 BC–18 AD)
(Archelaus was the son of Herod the Great)

2,401

About half.
Answer to "How many people work at the Vatican?"

—Pope John XXIII (1881–1963)

2,402

A stick.
Answer to "What do you call a boomerang that won't come back?"

—*Unknown*

2,403

I'm not sure.
Answer to "What is the Heisenberg uncertainty principle?"

—*Terry Pratchett in* The Fifth Elephant, *2000*

2,404

Five foot eleven.
Answer to "How long were you in the army?"

—*Spike Milligan (1918–2002)*

2,405

No, I just lie there.
Answer to "Do you have an active sex life?"

—*Unknown*

2,406

What's playing?

Answer to "Do you want to have sex or watch a movie?"

—*Bill Lee*

2,407

We've never been intimate.

Answer to "Do you believe in God?"

—*Noël Coward (1899–1973)*

2,408

A, B, C, D, E, F, G.

Carnac the Magnificent's answer to "What were some of the earlier forms of Preparation H?"

—*Johnny Carson (1925–2005)*

2,409

Hi, diddle-diddle.

Carnac the Magnificent's answer to "How do you greet your diddle-diddle in the morning?"

—*Johnny Carson (1925–2005)*

2,410

Rub a dub-dub.
Carnac's answer to "What does a masseuse do to your dub-dub?"

—*Johnny Carson (1925–2005)*

2,411

Only in mating season.
Answer to "Do you come here often?"

—*Spike Milligan (1918–2002)*

2,412

Denial.
Answer to "What state are we in?"

—Calvin and Hobbes *(Bill Watterson)*

2,413

Didn't you just ask me that?
Answer to "Have you ever had a feeling of déjà vu?"

—*Chet Hurley*

2,414

Let heaven and nature sing!
Answer to "Honey, I'm home!"

—*Cartoonist George Price (1901–1995)*

2,415

Oral Roberts.
Answer to "What do you call two gays named Bob?"

—Unknown

2,416

Do you mind if I get sick?
Answer to "Do you mind if I smoke?"

—Sir Thomas Beecham (1879–1961)

FACTS

2,417

If one sticks too rigidly to one's principles, one would hardly see anybody.

—*Agatha Christie (1890–1976)*

2,418

The point of quotations is that one can use another's words to be insulting.

—*Amanda Cross (1926–2003)*

2,419

The man who never makes a mistake gets tired of doing nothing.

—*Will Rogers (1879–1935)*

2,420

If you aren't ashamed once in a while, you aren't honest.

—*William Faulkner (1897–1962)*

2,421

Masquerading as a normal person day after day is exhausting.

—*Unknown*

2,422

When you live by yourself, all your annoying habits disappear.

—*Merrill Markoe*

2,423

Cowardice is often based on good information.

—*Peter Ustinov (1921–2004)*

2,424

Whatever temperature a room is, it's always room temperature.

—*Steven Wright*

2,425

No matter how good you get at tennis, you'll never be as good as a wall.

—*Mitch Hedberg (1968–2005)*

2,426

To achieve the impossible dream, try going to sleep.

—*Joan Klempner*

2,427

There's something about a closet that makes a skeleton restless.

—*Wilson Mizner (1876–1933)*

2,428

We are 68 percent water. That's how close to drowning we are.

—*Steven Wright*

2,429

Where facts are few, experts are many.

—*Donald R. Gannon*

2,430

Winter is reality, summer is illusion.

—*Toivo Pekkanen (1902–1957)*

2,431

You are not superior just because you view the world in an odious light.

—Vicompte de Chateaubriand (1768–1848)

2,432

We have only one person to blame, and that's each other.

—Barry Back

2,433

If you are afraid of being lonely, don't try to be right.

—Jules Renard (1864–1910)

2,434

Nothing is ever accomplished by a reasonable man.

—George Bernard Shaw (1856–1950)

2,435

Misquotations are the only quotations that are never misquoted.

—Hesketh Pearson (1887–1964)

2,436

Stoop and you'll be stepped on; stand tall and you'll be shot at.

—*Carlos A. Urbizo*

2,437

A stale mind is the devil's bread box.

—*Mary Bly*

2,438

Donald Trump has royal blood. His hair is a direct descendant of William of Orange.

—*Argus Hamilton*

2,439

We are inclined to believe those whom we do not know because they have never deceived us.

—*Samuel Johnson (1709–1784)*

2,440

There is no arguing with Johnson, for when his pistol misfires, he knocks you down with the butt.

—*Oliver Goldsmith (1730–1774)*

2,441

We learn from experience that we don't learn from experience.

—George Bernard Shaw (1856–1950)

2,442

Shaw is too much gasbag.

—D. H. Lawrence (1885–1930)

2,443

Instant gratification is not soon enough.

—From the movie Postcards from the Edge, *1990*

2,444

"Sort of" is a harmless thing to say, except after "I love you," "You're going to live," and "It's a boy."

—Demetri Martin

2,445

We forfeit three-fourths of ourselves to be like other people.

—Arthur Schopenhauer (1788–1860)

2,446

An expert is a person who has made all the mistakes that can be made in a very narrow field.

—Niels Bohr (1885–1962)

2,447

A clown isn't funny in the moonlight.

—Lon Chaney (1883–1930)

2,448

The sad truth is that excellence makes people nervous.

—*Shana Alexander (1925–2005)*

2,449

People who are late are usually jollier than the people who have to wait for them.

—*E. V. Lucas (1868–1938)*

2,450

To be good is noble, but to show others how to be good is nobler and less trouble.

—*Mark Twain (1835–1910)*

2,451

Procrastination gives you something to look forward to.

—*Joan Konner*

2,452

All aunts are alike. Sooner or later, out pops the cloven hoof.

—*P. G. Wodehouse (1881–1975)*

2,453

There is no such thing as a free association.

—Cindy Nelms

2,454

Never mind living well, revenge is the best revenge.

—Stefan Kanfer

2,455

The underdog is in a good position to bite.

—John Irving

2,456

If it weren't for erroneous conclusions, people would never reach any.

—Richard Russo

2,457

Occasionally we dance in our chains.

—Friedrich Nietzsche (1844–1900)

2,458

While there is no reason to panic, it is only prudent to make preparations to panic.

—*Cartoon caption by Robert Mankoff*

2,459

The KKK is so isolated now they are reduced to hating themselves.

—*Jay Leno*

2,460

A person's eyes reveal everything. They are the bicycle shorts of the soul.

—*Daniel Liebert*

2,461

Sit down naked on a wicker chair and your rear end will look like a giant Triscuit.

—*Daniel Liebert*

2,462

I tried being myself but it got me nowhere.

—*Cartoon caption by Mischa Richter (1910–1992)*

2,463

"Be yourself" is the worst advice you can give some people.

—*Tom Masson*

2,464

After many years of experience, I have come to the conclusion that you can't come to a conclusion.

—*Vita Sackville-West (1892–1962)*

2,465

Do not do unto others as you would have them do unto you—their tastes might not be the same.

—*George Bernard Shaw (1856–1950)*

2,466

Success and failure are equally disastrous.

—*Tennessee Williams (1911–1983)*

2,467

Why hate somebody for the color of their skin when there are many better reasons?

—*Unknown*

2,468

Intelligent statements never begin with the word "Dude."

—Demetri Martin

2,469

Friends are just enemies who don't have the guts to kill you.

—Judy Tenuta

2,470

Guilt is the price we willingly pay for doing what we are going to do anyway.

—Isabelle Holland (1920–2002)

2,471

Calamities are of two kinds: misfortune to ourselves and good fortune to others.

—Ambose Bierce (1842–1914)

2,472

A bigot is someone who hates different people than you do.

—Jerry Tucker

2,473

If you want to get rid of somebody, just tell him something for his own good.

—Kin Hubbard (1868–1930)

2,474

If it has tires or testicles, you're going to have trouble with it.

—Linda Furney

ASSORTED NUGGETS

2,475

The ability to delude yourself may be an important survival tool.

—*Jane Wagner*

2,476

Delusions of grandeur make me feel better about myself.

—*Jane Wagner*

2,477

When all else fails, there is always self-delusion.

—*Conan O'Brien*

2,478

I was born with a priceless gift, the ability to laugh at the misfortunes of others.

—*Dame Edna Everage (Barry Humphries)*

2,479

Everyone is entitled to my opinion.

—Ashleigh Brilliant (often misattributed)

2,480

You don't realize what life is all about until you are on the edge of a great abscess.

—Samuel Goldwyn (1882–1974)

2,481

When are you going to realize that if it doesn't apply to me, it doesn't matter?

—Candice Bergen in Murphy Brown

2,482

I lack the moral fiber to make enemies.

—Murray Kempton (1917–1997)

2,483

I have been selfish all my life in practice, though not in principle.

—Jane Austen (1775–1817)

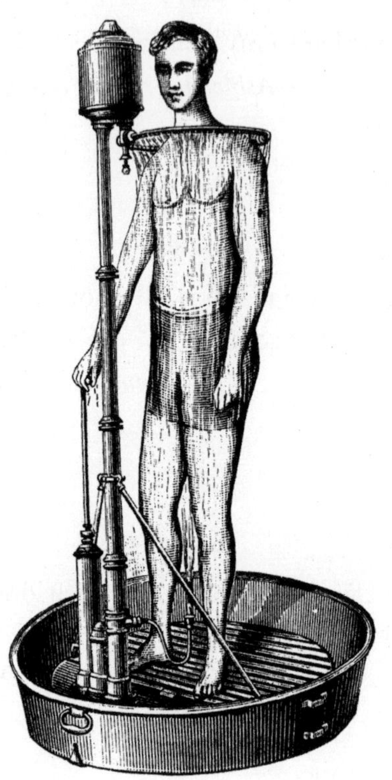

2,484

You know your party is out of control when people you don't even know ask you how the shower works.

—*Buddy Baron*

2,485

I have often depended on the blindness of strangers.

—*Adrienne Gusoff*

2,486

Kate Millet is an imploding beanbag of poisonous self-pity.

—Camille Paglia

2,487

Camille Paglia is a crassly egocentric, raving twit.

—Molly Ivins (1944–2007)

2,488

Since, as you say, Geoffrey, that we only pass this way but once, it seems a shame to be such a pompous ass.

—Cartoonist James Stevenson

2,489

Blame someone else and get on with your life.

—Alan Woods

2,490

I tend to live in the past because most of my life is there.

—Herb Caen (1916–1997)

2,491

So near and yet so what?

—*Unknown*

2,492

There is a television commercial where a customer has never heard of Preparation H. Where has he had his head?

—*Gallagher*

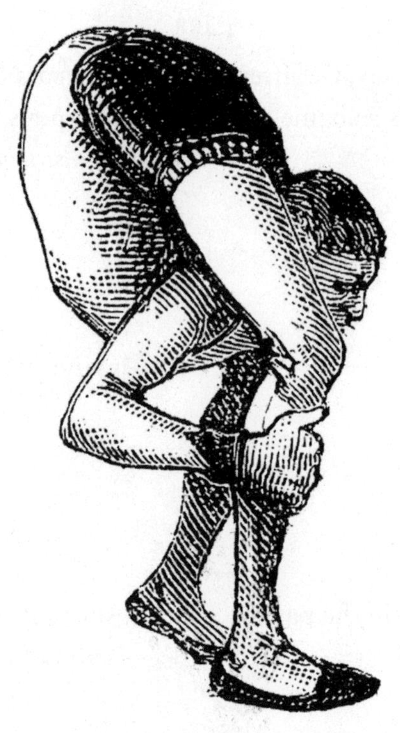

2,493

Walk a mile in another man's moccasins and you'll be a mile away and have his moccasins.

—Jack Handey

2,494

I've had a perfectly wonderful evening, but this wasn't it.

—Groucho Marx (1890–1977)

2,495

I fear nothing so much as a man who is witty all day long.

—Madame de Sévigné (1626–1696)

2,496

To shop at 7-Eleven these days you need to know the Hindu word for doughnut.

—David Brenner

2,497

It takes a big man to cry, and an even bigger man to laugh at him.

—Jack Handey

2,498

They say it takes more courage to walk away than to stand and fight. I wish somebody had told me that before I got my ass kicked.

—*John King*

2,499

I no longer use shampoo. Now I use real poo.

—*Jim Loy*

2,500

Before meditating I have an espresso to make it more challenging.

—*Betsy Salkind*

2,501

A guy said to me, "I'm sorry, I thought you were somebody else." I said, "I am."

—*Demetri Martin*

2,502

I came out of a handicapped stall in a men's room and somebody asked me if I was handicapped. I said, "No, but I was when I went in."

—*George Carlin (1937–2008)*

2,503

One of the nice things about gardening is that if you put it off long enough, it is too late.

—Bill Vaughan (1915–1977)

2,504

Vuja-de: the feeling that something never happened before.

—George Carlin (1937–2008)

2,505

It's the greatest thing since they reinvented unsliced bread.

—William Keegan

2,506

No man is an island, so don't tie your boat to a guy.

—Johnny Carson (1925–2005)

2,507

Is it weird in here or is it just me?

—Steven Wright

2,508

I've always been part of the lunatic fringe, but not an actual lunatic.

—*Cynthia Heimel*

2,509

Deep down, he's shallow.

—*Peter De Vries (1910–1993)*

2,510

Take a bath. You look like the second week of a garbage strike.

—*Neil Simon*

2,511

What if there was no such thing as a hypothetical question?

—*Dan Bradley*

2,512

I don't care about anything anymore. Yesterday, Jimmy cracked corn and I don't care.

—*Howie Mandel*

2,513

Wisdom from Bart Simpson:

A burp is not an answer.
Goldfish don't bounce.
Tar is not a toy.
High explosives and school don't mix.

—Matt Groening

2,514

I would like to apologize to the National Association for the Advancement of Colored People for referring to its members as "colored people."

—Steve Martin in Pure Drivel, *1998*

2,515

Whenever a friend succeeds, a little something within me dies.

—Gore Vidal

2,516

Today's headlines are tomorrow's pantry-shelf liners.

—Jazbo of Old Dubuque (J. P. Mulgrew, 1886–1949)

2,517

Meditation makes doing nothing respectable.

—Paul Dean

2,518

Coming are British the!

—Paul Reverse, Prairie Home Companion, *March 1999*

2,519

COME TO THE DARK SIDE—WE HAVE COOKIES.

—Bumper sticker

2,520

If you can't laugh at yourself, make fun of other people.

—Bobby Slayton

2,521

You have the soul of a winner. I mean *wiener.*

—From the TV series Cheers

2,522

I got my first laugh in a Laundromat when I obeyed a sign that said WHEN THE MACHINE STOPS, REMOVE ALL YOUR CLOTHES.

—*Phyllis Diller*

2,523

I'm not black, I'm alternatively hued. White people are melanin-impaired.

—*Ngaio Bealum*

2,524

I cried when I saw a man who had no shoes until I met a man who reminded me that we were at the beach.

—The Quigmans *(Buddy Hickerson)*

2,525

I cried because I had no shoes until I met a man who had no Odor-Eaters.

—*Ruth Parrish*

2,526

Knowledge is power, if you know it about the right person.

—*Ethel Watts Mumford (1878–1940)*

2,527

If you are a houseguest and you go upstairs to the bathroom and there is no toilet paper, you can always slide down the banister. Don't tell me you haven't done it.

—*Paul Merton*

2,528

Claustrophobia: fear of fat people in red suits.

—*Cynthia Louise Laffoon*

2,529

An ounce of pretension is worth a pound of manure.

—*Steven F. Clark*

2,530

A conscience is the inner voice that tells you that someone may be looking.

—*H. L. Mencken (1880–1956)*

2,531

Why do men have nipples? They're like plastic fruit.

—*Carol Leifer*

2,532

I can't be everything to everyone. Send me your specs.

—*Mo Rocca*

2,533

I once saw a forklift lift a crate of forks. It was way too literal for me.

—*Mitch Hedberg (1968–2005)*

2,534

The best way to make your dreams come true is to wake up.

—*Paul Valéry (1871–1945)*

2,535

Never forget that cologne is for after showering, not instead of showering.

—*Carol Leifer*

2,536

Never do anything virtuous until you minimize the damage it will cause.

—*Edgar Schneider*

2,537

A coward is a hero with a wife, kids, and a mortgage.

—Marvin Kitman

2,538

I got along famously with Prince Edward until I put that piece of ice down his neck.

—Lily Langtry (1853–1929)

2,539

We sold our house and are moving into one of those pandemoniums.

—Marie Aragon

2,540

Whenever I see an old lady slip and fall on a wet sidewalk, my first instinct is to laugh. But then I think, what if I was an ant and she fell on me? Then it wouldn't seem quite so funny.

—Jack Handey

2,541

When I buy plants at the nursery, I ask for something with a will to live.

—Greg Hahn

2,542

Whenever I try a different deodorant, for the rest of the day I feel like there's a stranger standing next to me.

—*Jim Gaffigan*

2,543

People only see Bigfoot at campgrounds and parks. He's clearly on vacation.

—*Darby Conley*

2,544

Diane: Hi, everybody! Guess why I'm here.
Carla: Generations of inbreeding?

—*From the TV series* Cheers

2,545

I stand before you as a plain, simple woman. The beautician can't take me until tomorrow.

—*Gracie Allen (1895–1964)*

2,546

Those who think they know it all are very annoying to those of us who do.

—*Sheetz's Rumination in* 1,001 Logical Laws, *1979, by John Peers*

2,547

Pretty redhead, thirty-three, wants semitraditional man. No nuevo-spiritualists, beach walkers, or minimum wagers. Prefer catcher's physique. 1B/3B/OF OK.

—LA Weekly, *October 25, 1990*

2,548

Transgendered person, male to female, seeks transgendered person, female to male, for possible foursome.

—*Cartoon caption by David Sipress*

NOTES AND INDEX OF SOURCES

The illustrations are taken mostly from fifteen collections of copyright-free drawings and clip art published by Dover Publications Inc., especially *Women*, *Men*, *Music*, *Food and Drink*, and *Love and Romance*, five books totaling more than three thousand line cuts, each with the subtitle *A Pictorial Archive from Nineteenth-Century Sources*. Another favorite trove was *Old Engravings & Illustrations, Volume One: People*, published by Dick Sutphen.

I spent many enjoyable hours leafing alternately through the quotes and the drawings looking for matches, and I was happy for minutes on end when I found a good one, such as those for quotes 93, 183, 1,610 (an amazing find), and 241, to name a few. In some cases, two drawings were combined, as in 313, 686, 721, and 1,332.

The quotes are mainly from the notebooks I've been keeping for years, some from other published collections, some from newspapers, magazines, comedy shows, and conversations, and a lot from the Internet. The nation's army of stand-up comedians is especially well represented in this compendium. Certain creative comics are rich sources of the kinds of one-liners I look for, the ones that don't require a setup or an explanation. I revere the comic skills of such old-time wits as Oscar Wilde, Mark Twain, Oscar Levant, Dorothy Parker, and Will Rogers, and moderns such as George Carlin, Steven Wright, Woody Allen, and the Queen of Quips, Rita Rudner, who could fill a book this size just with her own inventions. Don't miss her show the next time you're in Las Vegas.

Readers of my earlier books of quotations have contributed many gems I would otherwise have missed, and some sent me their own collections. I acknowledge them in notes below. Special thanks to Mardy Grothe, Adrienne Gusoff, Marty Indik, and others I have forgotten.

Television celebrities such as Johnny Carson, Jay Leno, David Letterman, Bill Maher, Jon Stewart, and Stephen Colbert are funny fellows, but they pose a problem for anyone trying to make proper ascriptions. Their need to have fresh material every night requires them to depend on teams of writers. Who knows who supplied any given zinger? Funny things said by actors, actresses, politicians, and public speakers are almost always the work of gag writers. As I have said before, I wish those gag writers would come forward and take credit for their work even if it costs them their jobs.

Want to know more about the people quoted and the things they have said? Google their names. That's what I did. This book would have been impossible to compile in less than a lifetime without Google and other search engines.

1. RC in the *Dubuque Telegraph Herald*, 9/16/06
2. DP in his *Bizarro* comic strip
3. Thanks to Liz Klinger
7. KM in *Gentlemen's Quarterly*, July 1990
36. JC as quoted in *Disraeli's Reminiscences*
55. RF on *Sanford and Son*
102. SdJ quoted by Herb Caen in the *San Francisco Chronicle*, 7/10/88
121. HR in *Rubaiyat of a Bachelor*
122. SJL in *Unkempt Thoughts*. Thanks to Lois Q. Novick
129. JT as Hank Kingsley on *The Larry Sanders Show*
157. RN in the 2010 documentary *The Nature of Existence*
188. Thanks to Thomas D'Elletto
206. TF on *Saturday Night Live*

252. Thanks to William Hicks
302. EO as quoted by Erica Jong in *Fear of Flying*
324. CD, *Pickwick Papers*
337. HLM in *A Little Book in C Major*
353. SS in *A Lie of the Mind*
365. PC in his 1991 movie *Hear My Song*
375. IM in the *Observer*, 2/4/68
378. Thanks to Valerie Donleavy
396. AJ was the sister of William and Henry James
417. Thanks to Linda Strauss
447. BH created the comic strip *The Lockhorns*
473. Thanks to Frank B. Miller
476. JW in *The Secrets of Harry Bright*
477. AB in the 1991 movie *Defending Your Life*
481. V in *Thoughts of a Philosopher*
502. DO on the *Tonight* show, 1/27/97
513. *The New Yorker*, 5/2/2011
559. Thanks to Paul Festa
590. EA in the 1945 movie *Mildred Pierce*
622. ED in *Reader's Digest*, 12/76
635. MR in the *Chicago Sun-Times*, 6/22/78
637. JBH in *The New Yorker*, 8/25/97
672. TE, obituary in *The New York Times*, 4/5/11
677. F quoted in *Frederick the Great* by Margaret Goldsmith
686. BW in his comic strip *Calvin and Hobbes*, 7/15/92
688. Thanks to Don Slattery
690. SS in the *Marin Independent Journal*, 2/16/92
694. JQ in *Gentlemen's Quarterly*, 7/90
720. PB in *The Ruling Class: A Baroque Comedy*, 1969
728. Thanks to Wally Rozak
744. Thanks to J. H. Dee
769. PP on HBO special *Women of the Night*, 1987
774. EE in *Back with a Vengeance*, 2004
786. Quoted by Herb Caen in the *San Francisco Chronicle*, 3/16/92
816. CMO was the third wife of Eugene O'Neill
824. From the play *Tru* by Jay Presson Allen
843. JP is the daughter of Abigail Van Buren
847. Thanks to Jonathan Benton
871. AC in *The Fall*, 1956
873. LR in *Maxims*, 1665
904. Thanks to John P. Allen
934. HJ in *Maxims of Books and Reading*, 1934

944. Thanks to Marty Indik
1,014. FL in *Metropolitan Life*
1,025. PB in her *I Hate to Cook Book*, 1960
1,064. FL in *Metropolitan Life*, 1974
1,103. ML on *Funny or Die*, 4/2011
1,191. JH in *The Book of Humor*, 2001
1,301. MT in *The Tragedy of Pudd'nhead Wilson*, 1894
1,306. Thanks to Andrew P. Campbell
1,321. WA in his 1966 movie *What's Up, Tiger Lily?*
1,322. *The New Yorker*, 2/10/77
1,351. Thanks to Jeffrey Bullock
1,373. RR in the *New York Herald Tribune*, 5/19/46
1,387. TF in *The New Yorker*, 2/14/11
1,388. BP, *365 Ink*, Dubuque, Iowa
1,392. Thanks to Susan Richman
1,396. MW in *The Psychotronic Encyclopedia of Film*, 1989
1,419. Thanks to Kathy Showen
1,421. GM in *Duck Soup*, 1933
1,456. SM in her comic strip *Shoe*, 1977
1,462. WHA in *Time*, 12/29/61
1,470. Thanks to Helen Giangregorio
1,481. Thanks to Blair Chotzinoff
1,488. *The New Yorker*, 1980
1,492. AH in *The Observer*, 8/17/69
1,503. ML quoted in the *San Francisco Chronicle*, 4/16/91
1,513. BML as quoted in *Forbes*, 4/4/91
1,630. SH in the *San Francisco Chronicle*, 5/29/94
1,653. RL in *The New Yorker*, 5/2/11
1,720. Thanks to Bea Quill
1,726. RM is cartoon editor of *The New Yorker*
1,745. Thanks to Marty Indik
1,751. Thanks to Bill Sauer
1,753. KL quoted in the *St. Louis Post-Dispatch*, 12/29/64
1,754. Thanks to Don Slattery
1,759. Thanks to R. T. Castleberry
1,760. JT quoted in the *San Francisco Chronicle*, 1/21/92
1,763. EL as quoted in *Never Trust a Calm Dog*, by Tom Parker, 1960
1,765. JM at the International Players Championship, 3/17/92
1,769. Thanks to Gordon DeWart
1,780. Thanks to Mel Graves
1,807. Thanks to Marty Indik
1,846. GW in a letter to Robert Howe, 8/17/1799

1,862. Thanks to Jonathan Benton
1,869. *The New Yorker*, 12/27/10
1,938. SDO at the American Bar Association convention, 1991
1,949. AB in *The Devil's Dictionary*, 1911
1,950. MPP in *A Glass Eye at the Keyhole*, 1938. Although MPP is often quoted, her birth and death dates are unknown even to Google.
2,015. RBR in a San Francisco speech
2,016. JH as quoted by Kurt Vonnegut
2,030. SF quoted in *The Life and Times of Sigmund Freud*, by Ernest Jones, 1957
2,040. DD was editor of *Unix World*
2,041. *The New Yorker*, 2/26/07
2,050. DG in *The Official Rules*, 1978
2,063. EB in *The House in Paris*, 1935
2,080. Thanks to Thomas D'Eletto
2,095. From the podcast *Stuff You Should Know*, 4/1/11
2,134. KM in *The Great Quotations*, 1960
2,153. FZ in *The Real Frank Zappa Book*, 1989
2,155. MR quoted in *Newsweek*, February 6, 1990
2,158. JO on his stand-up TV show, 4/28/11
2,168. PH on Comedy Central's *Hot List*, 12/5/10
2,169. JC on the *Tonight* show, 9/11/91
2,212. Thanks to Jonathan Benton
2,288. HB in an 1835 letter. Thanks to Frederick Gabrielsen
2,299. C in *The Blue Lantern*, 1949
2,305. PG was a professor and theologian at Harvard
2,306. JJ in *Lesbian Nation, the Feminist Solution*, 1973
2,319. JB on KNBR, San Francisco, 11/13/90
2,320. CD in his *Autobiography*, 1887. Omissions restored, 1958
2,322. PB is a British theater director
2,356. JBB in his syndicated column, 6/9/91
2,373. JM in his comic strip *Mr. Boffo*, 1994
2,436. CAU in a letter to Byrne
2,438. AH in his syndicated column, 5/3/11
2,490. HC in the *San Francisco Chronicle*, 4/11/91
2,535. CL in her 2009 book, *When You Lie About Your Age, the Terrorists Win*
2,543. DC in his comic strip *Get Fuzzy*
2,548. *The New Yorker*, 6/1/03

INDEX OF AUTHORS

(*Note:* Numbers refer to quotations, not pages.)

X

Y

Z

INDEX OF SUBJECTS AND KEY WORDS

(*Note:* Numbers refer to quotations, not pages.)

ABOUT THE AUTHOR

Viewed from the rear, Robert Byrne's head resembles a coconut and, when struck, emits a clear bell-like tone. The frequency is 440 cycles per second, better than an oboe for tuning an orchestra, a task he has performed on several memorable occasions. Core samples have shown that the inside of his head resembles a coconut as well.

The front view is dominated by the promontory of his nose, which is large enough to house part of his prefrontal cortex. During flu season he wears a Kevlar face mask to protect bystanders against a sneeze, which might blow his brains out.

Despite crippling emotional defects that have made him alternately pompous and sniveling, Byrne has managed to write seven novels, seven books on the games of pool and billiards, seven collections of quotations, and several other books whose titles don't immediately come to mind. In 2009 came a collection of his comic essays called *Behold My Shorts*, available from Amazon (the Internet site, not the river). His website is byrne.org.

After forty years in the San Francisco Bay Area as a magazine editor, he moved with his artist wife, Cynthia, to his hometown of Dubuque, Iowa, where the corn is as tall as an elephant's ball and authorities don't know what number to call.

(Note: The previous sentence can be sung to the tune of "Buckle Down, Winsocki.")